Inter text

The Language of Work

'*The Language of Work* is, without doubt, a valuable addition to the excellent Intertext series. Almut Koester combines intellectual rigour with accessibility and provides readers with an authoritative and coherent overview of language in the workplace. It is a skilful combination of essential knowledge and engaging and thought-provoking activities.'

Steve Cooper, *Principal Examiner AS/A2 English Language*, UK

'This book will provide students with a clear and useful introduction to the study of language in the world of work. It includes lots of appropriate examples and helpful self-study activities. It even ends on a practical note, with the last unit providing students with some linguistic insights into the job advertisements they are likely to deal with.'

Neil Mercer, *The Open University*, UK

The INTERTEXT series has been specifically designed to meet the needs of contemporary English Language Studies. *Working with Texts: A core introduction to language analysis* (second edition, 2001) is the foundation text, which is complemented by a range of 'satellite' titles. These provide students with hands-on practical experience of textual analysis through special topics, and can be used individually or in conjunction with *Working with Texts*.

The Language of Work:

◎ examines how language is used in business and the workplace, looking at a range of situations and data: from meetings to informal negotiations, promotional letters to emails

◎ explores representations of work in advertising, career magazines and workplace talk

◎ looks at the way people in business interact through small talk, politeness, customer care and management–employee relationships

◎ is illustrated with lively examples taken from the real world and includes a full index of terms

◎ features a useful section on entering the world of work, exploring job adverts and texts that give advice on CV writing and developing 'transferable skills'.

Almut Koester is a Lecturer in English Language at Birmingham University, UK.

The Intertext series

The Routledge INTERTEXT series aims to develop readers' understanding of how texts work. It does this by showing some of the designs and patterns in the language from which they are made, by placing texts within the contexts in which they occur, and by exploring relationships between them.

The series consists of a foundation text, *Working with Texts: A core introduction to language analysis*, which looks at language aspects essential for the analysis of texts, and a range of satellite texts. These apply aspects of language to a particular topic area in more detail. They complement the core text and can also be used alone, providing the user has the foundation skills furnished by the core text.

Benefits of using this series:

◎ **Multi-disciplinary** – provides a foundation for the analysis of texts, supporting students who want to achieve a detailed focus on language.

◎ **Accessible** – no previous knowledge of language analysis is assumed, just an interest in language use.

◎ **Student-friendly** – contains activities relating to texts studied, commentaries after activities, highlighted key terms, suggestions for further reading and an index of terms.

◎ **Interactive** – offers a range of task-based activities for both class use and self-study.

◎ **Tried and tested** – written by a team of respected teachers and practitioners whose ideas and activities have been trialled independently.

The series editors:

Adrian Beard was until recently Head of English at Gosforth High School, and now works at the University of Newcastle upon Tyne. He is a Chief Examiner for AS and A Level English Literature. He has written and lectured extensively on the subjects of literature and language. His publications include *Texts and Contexts* (Routledge).

Angela Goddard is Head of Programme for Language and Human Communication at the University College of York St John, and is Chair of Examiners for A Level English Language. Her publications include *Researching Language* (second edition, Heinemann, 2000).

Core textbook:

Working with Texts: A core introduction to language analysis
(second edition, 2001)
Ronald Carter, Angela Goddard, Danuta Reah, Keith Sanger and
Maggie Bowring

Satellite titles:

The Language of Advertising: Written texts
(second edition, 2002)
Angela Goddard

Language Change
Adrian Beard

The Language of Children
Julia Gillen

The Language of Comics
Mario Saraceni

The Language of Conversation
Francesca Pridham

The Language of Drama
Keith Sanger

The Lanquaqe of Fiction
Keith Sanger

Language and Gender
Angela Goddard and Lindsey Meân
Patterson

The Language of Humour
Alison Ross

*The Language of ICT: Information and
communication technology*
Tim Shortis

The Language of Magazines
Linda McLoughlin

The Language of Newspapers
(second edition, 2002)
Danuta Reah

The Language of Poetry
John McRae

The Language of Politics
Adrian Beard

*The Language of Speech and
Writing*
Sandra Cornbleet and
Ronald Carter

The Language of Sport
Adrian Beard

The Language of Television
Jill Marshall and Angela Werndly

The Language of Websites
Mark Boardman

The Language of Work
Almut Koester

The Language
of Work

Almut Koester

Routledge
Taylor & Francis Group

LONDON AND NEW YORK

First published 2004
by Routledge
2 Park Square, Milton Park, Abingdon, Oxon, OX14 4RN

Simultaneously published in the USA and Canada
by Routledge
270 Madison Ave, New York, NY 10016

Reprinted 2006, 2007

Transferred to Digital Printing 2009

*Routledge is an imprint of the Taylor & Francis Group,
an informa business*

© 2004 Almut Koester

Typeset in Stone Sans/Stone Serif by
Florence Production Ltd, Stoodleigh, Devon
Printed and bound in Great Britain by
TJI Digital, Padstow, Cornwall

British Library Cataloguing in Publication Data
A catalogue record for this book is available from the
British Library

Library of Congress Cataloging in Publication Data
Koester, Almut.
  The language of work/Almut Koester.
       p. cm. – (Intertext)
     1. Language and languages.   2. Business – Language.   I. Title.
  II. Series: Intertext (London, England)
  P41.K59 2004
  306.44 – dc 22   2003024420

ISBN 10: 0–415–30729–5 (hbk)
ISBN 10: 0–415–30730–9 (pbk)

ISBN 13: 978-0–415–30729–1 (hbk)
ISBN 13: 978-0–415–30730–7 (pbk)

contents

Acknowledgements ix
Notes on transcription xi

Unit one: Introduction to the language of work   **1**

Aims of this book   1
What is special about the language of work?   2
Variation in workplace language   7
Summary   11
Answers to the activities   11

Unit two: Perspectives on the world of work   **15**

Aims of this unit   15
How we perceive different professions   16
Discourse communities and their values   19
Work and the individual   21
Summary   23
Commentaries on the activities   24

Unit three: Written workplace genres   **29**

Aims of this unit   29
Written communication: letters, fax and email   30
Sales promotion letters   35
Flexibility and variation in genre   38
Written and spoken genres at work   43
Summary   47
Answers to the activities   48

Unit four: Spoken workplace genres   **53**

Aims of this unit   53
Meetings   53

Negotiating 57
Speakers' roles 60
Problem-solving 62
Instructions and procedures 66
Summary 69
Commentaries on the activities 71

Unit five: Relationships at work   77

Aims of this unit 77
Task goals and relational goals 77
Bosses and employees 79
Dealing with problems 83
Politeness and 'face' 85
Relationships with customers 85
Service encounters 88
Summary 93
Commentaries on and answers to the activities 94

Unit six: Entering the job market   101

Aims of this unit 101
Help with the job hunt 101
Written and spoken procedural genres 106
Job advertisements 108
Summary 110
Answers to the activities 111

References and further reading 117
Index of terms 121

acknowledgements

I'd like to thank all those people who let me use their 'voices' throughout this book, and those who gave permission for the letters, emails and the 'Conversation stoppers' text to be used in Unit three. And of course a big thanks to Terry for this support, as always, in this project.

Carter, R. and McCarthy, M., *Exploring Spoken English*, 1997, Cambridge University Press, extract from pp. 85–6, 'Students Chatting Round the Tea Table'. Reproduced by permission of Cambridge University Press.

Drew, H. and Heritage, J., *Talk at Work*, 1993, Cambridge University Press, extract by Christian Heath from p. 240. Reproduced by permission of Cambridge University Press.

'Case Study – Nursing', from *Opportunity: The Careers Magazine for Black and Asian Students*, vol. 3, no. 4, p. 13. Reproduced by permission of the *Independent*.

'The Fast Stream Development Programme' advertisement for the Inland Revenue, appeared in *Advantage: The Older Graduate's Career Guide*, November 2002. Reproduced by permission of the Inland Revenue.

'Emma Coghill: Teacher', from *Advantage: The Older Graduate's Career Guide*, November 2002. Reproduced by permission of Cherry Publishing Ltd.

'Workplace Conversations', from the Cambridge International Corpus. © Cambridge University Press.

Cheepen, C. 'Small talk in service dialogue: the conversational aspects of transactional telephone talk', 2000, from J. Coupland (ed.), *Small Talk*, extract from pp. 288–311. Reproduced by permission of Pearson Education.

'Ready for lift off?' by Ian Wylie, from the *Guardian*, 31 May 2003 © The Guardian 2003. Reproduced with permission. www.guardian.co.uk.

'Ask Rise', from the *Guardian*, 31 May 2003 © The Guardian 2003. Reproduced with permission. www.guardian.co.uk.

'FAQs', from *Prospects: Focus on Work Experience 2003*. Reproduced by permission of Graduate Prospects.

Every effort has been made to contact copyright holders. Any omissions brought to the attention of the publishers will be rectified in future editions.

notes on transcription

When looking at the transcripts of workplace conversations in this book, it is important to remember that these are not written texts, but an attempt to represent as accurately as possible in written form the way spoken language actually sounds. In order to reflect certain characteristics of speech, a number of special conventions are used:

(.)   noticeable pause or break of less than one second, with longer pauses indicated by the number of full seconds, e.g. (1), (2), (3);

–   sound abruptly cut off, e.g. false start;

italics   emphatic stress;

↑   a step up in pitch (speaker's voice becomes higher or louder);

↓   a drop in pitch (speaker's voice becomes lower or softer);

/?/   indicates inaudible utterances: one ? for each syllable;

⌐   overlapping or simultaneous speech;

⌐ ⌐   words in these brackets are utterances interjected by a speaker within another speaker's turn;

[ ]   words in these brackets indicate non-linguistic information, e.g. speakers' gestures or actions;

[. . .]   part of the text or conversation has been left out;

.hh   inhalation (intake of breath);

hhh   aspiration (releasing of breath).

Writing is structured in terms of sentences and punctuation, however speech is structured through **intonation**, that is through stress, pitch and rhythm. In order to highlight these differences between spoken and written language, capitalization is not used except for proper nouns, nor is punctuation, except to aid comprehension in certain cases: question marks to show the speaker is asking a question, exclamation marks for animated intonation, and full stops or commas to indicate how longer turns are structured. Although standard spelling is normally used, a certain number of words and expressions that frequently differ from their written forms such as *yeah* and *wanna*, are transcribed the way they are spoken. Hesitation markers, such as *uh* (*er*) or *uhm* (*erm*) are also transcribed.

Where no source is given for the transcript, it is from the author's data. For transcripts from other sources, transcription conventions of the source text have been used, except for some minor simplifications.

Introduction to the language of work

We spend a good part of our adult lives communicating at work. When we enter the world of work, we encounter many forms of spoken and written communication that are completely new to us, but, with time, we learn how to understand and use them ourselves. The language of work, therefore, plays an important role in the lives of most people. Even outside the workplace, people participate in professional inter-actions as customers, clients or patients: for example in interacting with doctors, solicitors, estate agents, banks etc. Most people are prob-ably aware that the way they communicate with friends and family is different in many ways from the way they communicate with their boss, a co-worker or a client. But they might not be able to say exactly which features distinguish workplace and professional language from more everyday language.

The aim of this book is to explore the distinctive features of the language used in professional and workplace settings. Workplace **discourse** is embedded in professional and organizational contexts, and involves communication between people in variety of relationships and roles, for example boss–employee, seller–customer etc. Therefore exam-ining workplace language will also involve looking at the roles played by these social contexts.

This unit provides a general introduction to the topic of the book, by trying to answer the following two questions:

1

1   What is special about the language of work?

2   How does the language of work vary in different workplace settings?

WHAT IS SPECIAL ABOUT THE LANGUAGE OF WORK?

According to Drew and Heritage (1992), 'institutional talk', as they call workplace and professional talk, differs from ordinary conversation in a number of ways:

◎   *Goal orientation*: participants in workplace conversations usually focus on specific tasks or goals.

◎   *Turn-taking rules or restrictions*: in some professional contexts (e.g. the courtroom) there are special **turn-taking** rules in operation. But even if no special rules exist, there may be unwritten restrictions on who speaks when; for example in doctor–patient consultations, it is the doctor who tends to ask the questions.

◎   *Allowable contributions*: there may be restrictions on what kinds of contributions are considered 'allowable', i.e. on what participants may say.

◎   *Professional lexis*: the professional/workplace context may be reflected in the lexical choice, i.e. in special **lexis** or vocabulary used by the speakers.

◎   *Structure*: workplace and professional interactions may be structured in specific ways.

◎   *Asymmetry*: workplace and professional interactions are often asymmetrical, that is often one speaker has more power and/or special knowledge than the other. Examples are conversations between a boss and an employee, or a doctor and a patient.

Note that although Drew and Heritage focus on the spoken language, all these distinguishing features of workplace language, except turn-taking rules and restrictions, also apply to the written language.

Look at the following two brief texts. The first, Text 1: Casual Conversation: Students Chatting Round the Tea Table, is from a casual conversation between students, and the second, Text 2: Workplace Conversation: Editorial Office, is from a workplace interaction. How are the two conversations different? Try to identify and note down differences relating to each of the six characteristics of workplace talk described above.

Text 1: Casual Conversation: Students Chatting Round the Tea Table

Three female students who share a house are having tea at home on a Sunday. Prior to the extract below, they have just been talking about food.

1	S03	I like Sunday nights for some reason, I don't know why
2	S02	[laughs] cos you come home
3	S03	I come home
4	S02	You come home to us
5	S01	and pig out
6	S02	Yeah yeah
7	S03	Sunday's a really nice day I think
8	S02	It certainly is
9	S03	It's a really nice relaxing day
10	S02	It's an earring, it's an earring
11	S03	⌊Oh lovely oh, lovely
12	S02	It's fallen apart a bit but
13	S03	It's quite a nice one actually, I like that, I bet, is that supposed to be straight?
14	S02	Yeah
15	S03	Oh I think it looks better like that
16	S02	And there was another bit as well, another dangly bit
17	S03	What, attached to
18	S02	⌊The top bit
19	S03	⌊That one
20	S02	Yeah . . . so it was even
21	S03	⌊Mobile earrings
22	S01	What, that looks better like that, it looks better like that

(Carter and McCarthy 1997: 86)

Text 2: Workplace Conversation: Editorial Office

Sally, an editor, is talking to her boss, Mary, in Mary's office. They have already been talking for some time about various work-related matters. Their conversation has just been interrupted by another person, who has now left.

1	Mary	sorry Sally
2	Sally	⌊I've got a couple more queries actually Mary then I'll leave you to get on
3	Mary	⌊yeah go ahead go ahead go ahead
4	Sally	um (.) oh just a quickie, when I'm doing a reprint
5	Mary	yeah
6	Sally	and I've got enough stock to last for about five months
7	Mary	yeah
8	Sally	what should I do? Just– get the estimate, saying that I don't need it for five months, or should I wait (.) should I (.)
		[. . .]
9	Mary	right ↑um (.) if it's not a front list key main (.) new (.) title
10	Sally	mm
11	Mary	I'd lower the reprint level
12	Sally	right
13	Mary	um (.) if it's something where there's a question mark as to whether you might go out of stock
14	Sally	yes, get it reprinted
15	Mary	⌊um (.)
16	Mary	ge– I'd get an estimate
17	Sally	yeah

4

Commentary

◎　**Goal orientation**

The speakers in the workplace conversation, Mary and Sally, clearly are focused on a specific goal: to answer Sally's query about reprints. It is more difficult to identify a goal for a casual conversation, where speakers seem to be involved in simply chatting, except perhaps the very general goal of social bonding. The conversation moves easily from topic to topic, for example from talking about how nice Sundays are to commenting on an earring that they find on the floor.

◎　**Turn-taking rules or restrictions**

In this professional context, an informal meeting in an office, there are no special turn-taking rules. Nevertheless, it is noticeable that the turn-taking is much 'tidier' than in the casual conversation. In Turns 1–8, Sally asks a question, and Mary acknowledges her 'listenership' with brief responses such as *yeah*. This pattern is inverted from Turns 9–17, when Mary answers the question, and Sally now 'listens actively', e.g. saying *right*. The students' conversation seems much more disjointed, with speakers freely making observations or commenting on what someone else has said. The turn-taking is very loosely structured, with frequent overlaps between turns, and speakers often completing each other's utterances, for example:

```
17   S03   What, attached to
18   S02                      ⌊The top bit
```

Although in the workplace conversation there is also some overlapping speech between turns, the roles of speaker and listener are much more clearly distinguishable.

◎　**Allowable contributions**

As the students know each other well, their conversation is very informal, and there do not seem to be any restrictions on what they can say. As noted above, the topic is not fixed, and in fact changes quite abruptly in Turn 10. The use of colloquialisms (e.g. *pig out*) is acceptable, and turns may be grammatically incomplete or the grammar may change mid-utterance, for example in the middle of Turn 13, where the speaker initiates a statement with *I bet*, and then decides to ask a question instead (*is that supposed to be straight?*).

Although the language is quite informal in the office conversation, for example Sally using the colloquialism *a quickie*, the speakers do not stray from the topic, and they seem to be paying more attention to their language.

Their utterances are grammatically more complex, with the use of subordinate clauses (e.g. *when I'm doing a reprint . . . what should I do?*), and they both make an effort to be polite. Sally begins by apologizing (Turns 2 and 4) for taking up Mary's time with her query: *I've got a couple more queries actually Mary then I'll leave you to get on / oh just a quickie.* Mary shows politeness by using an indirect form in telling Sally how to do the job: in Turn 11 she uses the conditional form (*I'd lower the reprint level*) rather than an imperative (*lower the reprint level*).

◎ **Professional lexis**

The professional context of the editorial office is reflected in a number of lexical items which are specific to publishing: *reprint, front, key, main title.* Other words more generally reflect the business context, and would be found in other workplace contexts: *stock, estimate.* Such use of professional jargon can make a **text** like this quite difficult to understand for non-professionals.

◎ **Structure**

As noted above, the office conversation has a clear turn-taking pattern, which contributes to its overall structure. It seems that one speaker always has longer turns (either asking or answering a question), while the other speaker makes brief acknowledging contributions. It is much more difficult to identify a clear overall structure in the students' conversation, although it would be wrong to say that it is unstructured. There are noticeable 'micro-structures' between turns, for example when speakers echo each others' utterances:

> 3   S03 I come home
> 4   S02 You come home to us

Another way in which the workplace conversation is structured is that Sally states clearly in Turn 2 what she wants to talk about: *I've got a couple more queries.* This kind of **metalanguage** (language about language) is quite common in workplace conversation, as it is a way to refer to the goal of the conversation. As casual conversations do not usually have such clear goals, metalanguage like this is more unusual; in fact it would seem strange in a casual conversation to announce what you are going to talk about.

◎ **Asymmetry**

The workplace conversation is an example of an asymmetrical interaction between a boss (Mary) and a subordinate (Sally). It is also asymmetrical in terms of knowledge and experience: Mary obviously knows more about the business and has more experience than Sally does. Both kinds of asymmetry are reflected in the interaction: the speakers work with the assumption that Mary has both the authority and knowledge to tell Sally what she should do. The student conversation, on the other hand, is between equals, but it is noticeable that not all speakers contribute equally to the talk: S02 and S03 speak much more than S01 does. So even casual conversations can have more subtle forms of asymmetry.

VARIATION IN WORKPLACE LANGUAGE

The above six characteristics of workplace language try to distinguish between casual conversation and workplace conversation in general. But, of course, the language in each sector of work has its own particular characteristics, and involves written as well as spoken interaction. As we saw in the last section, each profession has its own special lexis. In addition, different workplace texts may also use specific grammar and sentence structure, and may vary in style. The set of linguistic features which characterizes texts in different professional contexts is known as **register**. So, for example, the register of the medical profession will be different from that of sales.

In addition to register, another important concept to explain variation in workplace language is that of **genre**. Each area of work uses a variety of spoken and written interactions in order to accomplish different things. Just as in literature, different literary categories are referred to as genres (for example novels, poems, plays), we can use the term 'genre' to refer to different types of spoken or written texts. For example in the legal profession, some of the spoken and written genres used are lawyer–client consultations, cross-examination, cases and judgements. According to Bhatia (1993: 13) a genre is:

> a recognizable communicative event characterized by a set of communicative purpose(s) identified and mutually understood by the members of the professional or academic community in which it regularly occurs.

This quote shows that a genre is defined first of all by its goal or purpose. In addition, as it occurs regularly and must be 'mutually understood', it usually has a predictable structure.

Activity

Look at the following spoken or written texts taken from different professional contexts and try to answer the following questions:

◎　What is the professional context?

◎　What genre is the extract?

◎　Who are the speakers or writers and readers and what are their roles?

◎　What clues in the text, including the structure, vocabulary, grammar and **style** (formal or informal), helped you identify the register and genre?

◎　If the text is incomplete, what part (beginning, middle or end?) is shown and what parts are missing?

◎　What is the communicative goal or purpose of the genre?

Text 3: Extracts from Different Professional Contexts

Extract 1

[. . .]

I hope that you are not too disappointed at the outcome and trust that this will not deter you from applying for any further vacancies with us in the future.

I would like to take this opportunity to thank you for your application and for the interest you have shown [. . .]

Extract 2

	[. . .]
Jim	yeah um– let's let's come up to date and uh (.) um (.)
Liz	by Thursday
Jim	by Thursday
Liz	Thursday at eleven. brilliant
Jim	let's see where we are and what's doing (.) an' (.) you know what needs (.) urgent attention
Liz	yes /?/ smashing

8

Extract 3

1 Apologies
2 **Minutes** of the Last Meeting
3 Matters Arising
4 Director's Items
5 Reports:
>   Summer Courses (JR)
>   Insessional (GM)
>   Business English Courses (CH)
6 Any Other Business
7 Date of Next Meeting

Extract 4

> [. . .]
A   hhhh You've got erm (0.8) bronchitis
B   er
>   (4.5) ((A begins to write prescription))
A   hhh (0.3) I'll give you antibiotics to take for a week hhh
>   (0.8)
B   How long are you here for?
A   We go back on Saturday
> [. . .]

(from Heath 1992: 240)

Check your answers at the end of this unit (pp. 11–13), then read the commentary below.

Commentary

Some of the genres were probably easy to identify, for example the doctor–patient interaction, as this is a genre you have probably taken part in yourself. Others might have been more difficult, such as the **agenda** of the meeting, as you may never have attended a formal meeting, and therefore would not have come across such a document before. This illustrates

Bhatia's point (in his definition above of genre) that genres are 'identified and mutually understood' by members of the professional community that use them. So the more familiar you were with the genres in the extracts, the easier it was for you to identify them. Even if you haven't used or encountered some of the genres yourself, you may be familiar with them because of indirect exposure through parents and friends, or through films and television. Maybe you also noticed that some of the genres are very specific to certain professional contexts, for example the general practice consultation, whereas others are used across a range of professional contexts, such as the spoken genre of arranging a meeting or the written agenda of a meeting.

The clues in the extracts which helped you to identify the register (i.e. the professional context) and the genre were probably of two types:

1   General features of the style and layout (in the case of a written text) or the style/level of formality and turn-taking structure (in the case of a spoken extract). For example, the agenda of a meeting has a very particular layout, basically consisting of a list of items.

2   Specific vocabulary and grammar relating to the register and genre, for example words such as *applying*, *vacancies*, *application* in the letter of refusal to the applicant, or the exclusive use of nouns in the agenda of the meeting.

This illustrates the point that genres have recognizable linguistic features, including special vocabulary and grammar, and characteristic overall structures. The interactive structure and style of the genre is greatly influenced by the roles of the speakers and writers/readers. For example, both spoken genres (Extracts 2 and 4) are asymmetrical, that is, one of the speakers plays a dominant role (the professor in Extract 2 and the doctor in Extract 4), which is reflected in the turn-taking structure. However, the styles of the two encounters are quite different: Extract 2 (arranging a meeting) is 'chatty' and informal, with speakers using words like *brilliant* and *smashing*, Extract 4 (the doctor–patient consultation) is more neutral and factual. This has to do with the fact that the **social distance** between the doctor and patient is much greater than between the professor and secretary. The professor and secretary are colleagues who work together on a regular basis, and, as in many offices, communication between them is very friendly and informal. In comparison, not only do the doctor and the patient have less frequent contact, but the doctor has a much more powerful position in relation to the patient. In our society, doctors command great respect, and wield tremendous power over their patients, which is reflected in the communication style between the two participants.

You may also have been able to identify which parts of the genre were shown and which were missing, for example the doctor–patient extract shows the diagnosis and prescription of treatment, but not the examination of the patient which came before. This shows that genres usually have beginnings, middles and ends, that is they often go through a number of stages. Finally, the activity should also have brought out the fact that it is the goal or purpose of the text or interaction which determines and shapes the genre. The communicative goal of the genre may even be reflected in its name, for example 'arranging a meeting' or 'letter of refusal'.

SUMMARY

This unit has identified some general characteristics of workplace texts and interactions:

◎   workplace language differs systematically from everyday language in a number of ways (six distinguishing features were identified);

◎   the language in different workplace and professional contexts varies in terms of the register it uses and the genres that occur.

The other units in this book will explore specific aspects of the language of work and the social contexts which surround it.

ANSWERS TO THE ACTIVITIES

Answers for Text 3: Extracts from Different Professional Contexts (pp. 8–9)

Extract 1

◎   Professional context: Personnel or Human Resources.

◎   Genre: letter of refusal to a job applicant.

◎   Writer: head of personnel or deputy in the Personnel or Human Resources department of an organization.

11

◎ Reader: a job applicant.

◎ Clues in the text:
  – the formal style indicates a very formal type of business letter;
  – vocabulary: *disappointed at the outcome, applying, vacancies, application.*

◎ Part shown: the end of the letter.

◎ Parts missing: the first part of the letter informing the applicant that he or she was not successful, and the opening and closing of the letter.

◎ Communicative goal or purpose: to inform the applicant that he or she has not been successful.

Extract 2

◎ Professional context: a university office (but could be any professional context).

◎ Genre: arranging a meeting.

◎ Speakers: a professor and a secretary (could be any hierarchical relationship).

◎ Clues in the text:
  – Jim seems to play a dominant role in arranging the meeting, which indicates that he is higher up in the hierarchy;
  – vocabulary: words referring to dates/times, e.g. *Thursday at eleven*;
  – grammar: the use of *let's* to refer to joint action to be taken.

◎ Part shown: the end of the encounter, where participants confirm the arrangements. This is shown by the repetition of the day and time, as well as comments like *brilliant* and *smashing*, which are typically used in closing conversations like this.

◎ Parts missing: the beginning and middle stages of arranging a meeting, where speakers propose and negotiate a day and time to meet.

◎ Communicative goal or purpose: to arrange a mutually acceptable time to meet in order to discuss a particular topic or do some work.

Extract 3

◎ Professional context: the English Language Teaching Unit of a university (could also be a language school).

◎ Genre: agenda of a meeting.

◎ Writer: head of department who will chair the meeting.

◎ Readers: members of the department, who will attend meeting.

◎ Clues in the text:

   – the layout of the text as a list of items;

   – vocabulary: *apologies, minutes, meeting, matters arising, any other business, courses, insessional, Business English*;

   – grammar: the exclusive use of nouns (e.g. *apologies*) and no verbs, except one gerund, *arising*.

◎ Part shown/parts missing: the entire text is shown except the heading, which includes the name of the department, the date, time and venue of the meeting.

◎ Communicative goal or purpose: to inform the participants what the meeting will be about.

Extract 4

◎ Professional context: medical.

◎ Genre: a general practice consultation.

◎ Speakers: a doctor (A) and a patient (B).

◎ Clues in the text:

   – the turn-taking structure, with (A) playing a dominant role (for example by asking questions), is typical of doctor–patient interactions;

   – vocabulary: *bronchitis, prescription, antibiotics*;

   – grammar: typical verb forms for the diagnosis (*you've got . . .*) and the prescription (*I'll give you . . .*).

◎ Part shown: the diagnosis and prescription of treatment.

◎ Parts missing: the first part of the interaction, where the doctor examines the patient, and the opening and closing of the encounter.

◎ Communicative goal or purpose: to diagnose the patient and prescribe a treatment for the complaint or illness.

Perspectives on the world of work

AIMS OF THIS UNIT

Once you start work, you become a member of a professional community, which has a set of professional practices and shares specialist knowledge and certain values. Language plays a key role here, as people working together in the same organization or field have mechanisms of intercommunication and use professional genres and specialist lexis. Linguists refer to such professional groups as **discourse communities** in order to emphasize the important role language plays in their constitution (see Swales 1990).

The aim of this unit is to explore the way in which the values and attitudes of a professional discourse community are reflected in the texts it uses. We will also look at the values and attitudes of people outside the professional community towards different professions, and at the relationship between the individual and the world of work.

HOW WE PERCEIVE DIFFERENT PROFESSIONS

Activity

What stereotypes are associated with the following professions and the type of language they use? For example, are people in these professions perceived as trustworthy, interesting, intelligent, articulate etc.?

◎   estate agents

◎   nurses

◎   computer programmers

◎   academics

◎   farmers

(See the commentary at the end of this unit, p. 24.)

Activity

Look at the following two texts. The first one, 'Case Study – Nursing' appeared in a special edition on nursing of a careers magazine for Black and Asian students. It is written in the first person by a senior nurse (whose name and place of work are given in the original). The second one, 'Inland Revenue' is a job advertisement for a tax specialist from the *The Older Graduate's Career Guide*. Before you read the texts, note down any stereotypes you would associate with the jobs of nurse and a tax specialist in the Civil Service. Then read the texts and answer the following questions:

◎   How do the texts try to dispel the stereotypes commonly associated with these professions?

◎   What language is used in order to do this and to make the work sound appealing?

Text 4: Case Study – Nursing

MY JOB involves making an assessment as to whether a patient is suitable for anti-coagulation therapy, which aims to prevent strokes, and then monitoring the patient.

It's a potentially dangerous drug, so the whole picture of their life has to be looked at very carefully and on an ongoing basis. I also deal with patients with thrombosis. I have 2,500 patients altogether. I'm also involved in a consultancy role, advising doctors and liaising with local hospitals when the patient is having other treatment. Again, that's because it's a dangerous drug.

In addition, I'm involved in education. I devised the first-ever anti-coagulation course and I have nurses from all over the UK attending. We'll shortly be releasing the first anti-coagulation nurse consultant in the UK. So it's an exciting time.

I always wanted to go into nursing. It was a passion and I was particularly interested in elderly care. It's a varied, autonomous and caring job which gives me huge satisfaction. Time and time again, I get rewarding letters from patients.

One that arrived last week said our service was incredibly efficient and professional. Given the perceived state of the NHS at the moment, that was a real buzz. In fact, if anyone asks me what my greatest achievement is in nursing, I don't say winning the awards that I have or even setting up the course. Rather, it's the satisfaction of providing the highest quality care possible for my patients.

Being black hasn't been an issue for me. Once people realised my skills and abilities, that was all that mattered and that's what opened doors for me.

I'm well respected and my development is still continuing.

(See the commentary at the end of this unit, pp. 24–5.)

Text 5: Inland Revenue

The Fast Stream Development Programme

Social inclusion,
child poverty,
the environment,
human rights.

Anyone else would find it too taxing

Helen Smith – MSc in Political Philosophy, LSE

Our IR Fast Stream takes you straight into the Policy division, and to the heart of political decision-making. It's here that we work with the strategies behind the country's tax system and other Revenue services like tax credits, the minimum wage and student loans.

Join us and you'll have the chance to work on live projects that contribute to key issues and bring about beneficial change in society.

Much of your focus will be on making sure taxation achieves everything the Government wants. During the Programme you could also simplify legislation, bring in new systems or identify different ways to make us more effective and accessible.

Much of what you do will demand consultations with customers and lobby groups, as well as meetings with Ministers, tax experts and specialists of all kinds. It will be important to hold your own in these high level meetings and discussions – which will take an independent spirit, courage to work differently, and confidence to say what you see through your fresh

eyes. It will be daunting, but there'll be so much support and training that you'll never feel out on a limb.

All appointments are London based and starting salaries for those following the Programme are currently £20,150 - £25,850. If you're a UK national with or expecting to achieve a second class honours degree in any discipline and you're ambitious to operate at the highest levels, please call Capita RAS for a brochure on 01325 745539. Ref: A03/0015/OIR or apply directly online at www.faststream.gov.uk

For more information call 01159 740604.
www.inlandrevenue.gov.uk/recruitment
At the Inland Revenue, we welcome applications from people of every kind of background, so that our own workforce mirrors the community we serve.

FASTSTREAM

(See the commentary at the end of this unit, pp. 25–6.)

DISCOURSE COMMUNITIES AND THEIR VALUES

The main aim of the two texts we have examined is to attract those making career choices into these professions, which are therefore described in highly favourable terms. These texts also give us some insights into the values of the professional community and the aims they pursue: *providing the highest quality care possible*, in the case of the nursing profession, and *making sure taxation achieves everything the Government wants*, in the case of the Inland Revenue text.

Text 6: Problematic Sales Rep (p. 20) is quite different, as it does not involve an idealized portrayal of the profession, but is a transcript of a real workplace conversation that took place in a small private business in the US. The text, in fact, describes a problematic situation: a sales rep who is not performing well. But such a negative portrayal of a work situation also gives us insights into the values of the discourse community and of the expectations it has of its workforce. The text shows extracts of a conversation in which the sales manager describes to the president of the company how he has been dealing with this problematic sales rep. The sales rep is in 'inside sales', that is he sells over the telephone, and the sales manager has been listening in on his telephone conversations with customers and then giving him feedback. The text consists mainly of reported speech: a repetition of what the sales manager claims to have said to the sales rep. For ease of reference, the sales manager's monologue is broken up into numbered segments.

Activity

Read Text 6: Problematic Sales Rep and answer the following questions, giving specific examples from the text:

◎ From what the sales manager says, what would you say is expected of a 'good' sales rep?

◎ What perception of the relationship between a manager and a subordinate is reflected in what the sales manager says?

◎ What does the text tell you about the way in which knowledge and expertise is acquired in this profession?

◎ What general values and assumptions about the sales profession does the text reflect?

Text 6: Problematic Sales Rep

1   yeah this morning. I (.) took him to Amy's office an' talked to him. .hh that he
      has (.) I says you've got (.) ↑ the work ethic ↓ you got the ↑ personality ↓ and
      you got the (.) uh (.) ↑ *ability* the– to do very well. and you are supposed to
      have some knowledge that you're coming *with* us

2   and that (.) since you been here in monitoring you have I– we've had several–
      conversations and we've had a spat (.) back and forth of things about (.) .hh
      what's happening and where are *you are* an' hh uh (.) ↓ then I says I– as your
      (.)↑supervisor I have to *tell* you that your per*form*ance is not what it *should* be.
      an' I have (.) been monitoring you, I have– every time I listen to you I write
      down things

3   an' we've discussed them more than once. an' these are re*curr*ing *things* that
      are happening. I says whether you stay at *this* company or go somewhere *else*,
      but (.) if you don't *deal* with these things you're not gonna succeed. I sa–
      oddly enough the things that are happening to you, what's happening are
      almost the– the top ten *reas*ons why people *fail*
      [. . .]

4   an' I been twenty years in selling (.) *ad*vertising an' *twelve* of that is *trade*
      advertising you know of *post*card decks. an' so I says if– I know, I don't even
      have to pick up the other side of the phone, I *know*, I can *tell* where you are
      an' what you're saying. a– I says but I *pick* up the side of the phone an' I take
      notes an' then I talk to you about it an' you tell me that that's not true
      [. . .]

5   yeah I says so I know I understand you re*ceive* what I say but you've not (.)
      applied what I say, an' you're assuming that you know more than *I* do. An' I
      says if that were *true* you would be producing sales an' (.) so (.) I says now I
      want you to come in *Mon*day an' tell me one way or another. are you ready to
      really go *after* it an' make a change?

6   or (.) an' you're willing to receive the instruction an' apply it, or are you just
      feeling oh this is over with an' it's not gonna go anywhere. an' say it's up to
      you. I says ↑ I'll be there to work with you *right* along side of you to make it
      happen if you want it to happen. but I've gotta see sig*nif*icant *change* in the
      next two weeks ↓or you're not gonna be with this company

(See the commentary at the end of this unit, pp. 26–7.)

WORK AND THE INDIVIDUAL

In Western cultures the individual plays a central role, and this is reflected in the way people talk and write about work. A job or profession is not usually seen merely as something you have to do to earn money and pay the bills, but as a 'career choice'. There is an expectation that the work you do should be personally fulfilling. Texts about work, therefore, often take the form of a personal narrative; for example, Text 4: Case Study – Nursing, which we looked at earlier.

Activity

Text 7: Teacher (from the *Older Graduate's Career Guide*) involves the personal narrative of a woman who changed her career from investment banking to teaching because she did not find her first job satisfying. Read through the text and the notes that follow. The paragraphs have been numbered for ease of reference.

Text 7: Teacher

1   Emma Coghill spent ten years in a job she hated, before enrolling on a degree course as a mature student. Although the 27 year old was on a high salary working on the trading floor of an investment bank, she hated the long hours and craved a new challenge.

2   "The money was great but I was bored out of my mind," she says. "I used to dread going to work every day. The hours were so long – I'd get to the office at 6.30am and never leave before 8pm. I felt absolutely brain-dead."

3   After leaving school without qualifications and joining the bank

21

aged 16, Emma gave up work in the City at 24. After taking her A-levels in evening courses, she enrolled on a full-time BA degree in Education at Middlesex University. She's never looked back.

4   "I found myself sitting in lectures and enjoying myself for the first time. Before I went to university I thought I was the only person who'd done a job for 10 years and hated it, but when I got to Middlesex I met loads of bankers, all in the same boat, who'd decided to make a career change as well."
[. . .]

5   Emma graduated this year with a first class degree. She is now working as a primary school teacher at a Coppice school in Hainault, London where she took one of her degree placements.

6   Although she is earning a third of her salary as an investment banker, she is enjoying the benefits of her new lifestyle and loves the challenge of working in a classroom.

7   "I wouldn't say teaching is an easy profession," she says. "In fact I would say it's harder than working in banking. But it's more flexible. I can leave school at 4pm and take my work home with me. It means I can do something I enjoy and also have a social life."

8   Age has never been an issue for Emma. "The children just see you as an adult and don't judge you in terms of how old you are," she explains. "And as for my colleagues, quite a few people go into teaching at a later age. It's not like I'm one amongst a load of 18 year olds."

9   Emma believes the benefits of having her degree far outweigh the monetary setbacks. The degree offered a chance for her to re-establish her career.
[. . .]

10   Emma loves education so much now that she's considering one day studying to become an educational psychologist.

Notes

In order to explain the reasons for her career change, notice how the narrator contrasts Emma's previous job in banking with her new one as a teacher. This is often done by using contrasting lexical items and parallel grammatical structures, for example:

   ◎   Although the 27 year old was on a high salary working on the trading floor of an investment bank, she hated the long hours and craved a new challenge (paragraph 1).

◎ Although she is earning a third of her salary as an investment banker, she is enjoying the benefits of her new lifestyle and loves the challenge of working in a classroom (paragraph 8).

Notice how the contrast between the two jobs is emphasized by repeating the same grammatical structure (beginning with a subordinate clause introduced by *although*) and some of the same key lexis (*salary, challenge*), as well as contrasting other lexical items:

◎ 'high salary' vs 'a third of her salary';

◎ 'hated' vs 'enjoying' and 'loves';

◎ 'working on the trading floor' vs 'working in the classroom'.

This is an example of a **matching contrast** relationship between two parts of a text (see Hoey 2001). Such parts can be adjacent sentences or even within the same sentence, or they may even be quite far removed from one another in the text, as in the above example.

Now see if you can find other examples of matching contrast relationships. Make a note of the contrasting sections of text, underlining the repetitions and contrasting items.

When you have finished, check your findings against the commentary at the end of this unit, pp. 27–8.

SUMMARY

This unit has explored the theme of how language expresses the values and attitudes associated with the workplace and with specific professions. This has included looking at perceptions of different professions from within the discourse community as well as from without. Our perceptions of different professions are influenced by stereotypes, and we have seen that organizations may try to counter such stereotypes in attracting new members into their profession. We have also examined general perceptions of the role of work in our lives, focusing on the importance placed on the individual.

Extension

1 Find representations of different jobs and professions in the media and analyse the way in which people in these professions are portrayed. You could look at advertisements or commercials which show people at work, comic strips, such as 'Dilbert' or job advertisements. Look in particular at whether the advertisement, commercial or strip draws on any stereotypes associated with the job. If so, are the stereotypes reinforced, or is there an attempt to challenge them?

2 Devise a questionnaire to interview people about their attitude towards one or more jobs/professions, and interview at least four different people. You could include some of the following questions:

◎ Do you think the job of X is important/interesting/challenging?

◎ Which qualities do you need to become a(n) X: intelligence, communication skills, patience?

◎ Have you ever considered becoming a(n) X? Why or why not?

COMMENTARIES ON THE ACTIVITIES

Commentary on stereotypes and professions (p. 16)

The stereotypes you came up with probably included the popular conception of estate agents as untrustworthy or even sleazy, and computer programmers as socially awkward and monosyllabic. Farmers are often perceived as not being particularly educated and as speaking with a regional dialect, and academics as using unnecessarily complex and obfuscating language, as well as having a great deal of free time on their hands. Organizations and companies trying to recruit young people to these professions often have to contend with such popularly-held stereotypes.

Commentary on Text 4: Case Study – Nursing (p. 17)

Nursing is often thought of as a fairly menial kind of job, which involves repetitive work and allows little scope for initiative. The text tries to dispel this stereotype by showing that the job of senior nurse involves variety (patient care, dealing with doctors and hospitals, education), as well as a high degree of responsibility and initiative, expressed through such lexical items as *assessment, monitoring, dangerous drug, consultancy, advising, devised (a) course*. The usual perception of nursing as a 'caring profession' is not mentioned until the fourth paragraph (*caring job*), but the adjective *caring* is only the last in a list of three describing the job: *a varied, autonomous and caring job*. In addition to such lexical items which highlight the variety and responsibility of the job, the work is also made to sound appealing by describing it as personally or emotionally satisfying, especially in the fourth and fifth paragraphs:

- exciting time
- It was a passion
- huge satisfaction
- rewarding letters
- a real buzz

Commentary on Text 5: Inland Revenue (p. 18)

A career in the Civil Service is usually thought of as secure, but rather dull, and most people would think of the work of a tax specialist as complicated but not particularly interesting. In addition, the Inland Revenue is often perceived as an unwelcome meddler in people's private affairs. The advertisement challenges both of these stereotypes. The headline of the advertisement seems to assert that far from meddling, the Inland Revenue is concerned with important social issues: *social inclusion, child poverty, the environment, human rights*. This is emphasized throughout the text, for example in the second paragraph: *contribute to key issues and bring about beneficial change in society*. The advertisement also tries to dispel the stereotype of this type of work as boring, and describes it as challenging and requiring initiative:

- it will be important to hold your own
- it will take independent spirit, courage to work differently and confidence . . .

The active role to be played by the tax specialist is also emphasized by the grammatical structure of the second sentence in the third paragraph, which consists of a series of transitive verbs (verbs requiring objects) which have the addressee (*you*) as subject:

◎   *you* could also *simplify* legislation, *bring* in new systems or *identify* different ways to . . .

Commentary on Text 6: Problematic Sales Rep (p. 20)

In segment 1 the sales manager lists a number of characteristics which he deems to be important for the job, and which he also believes the sales rep to possess: *work ethic, the personality, the ability to do well*. However, the sales rep's *performance is not what it should be* (segment 2), and in segment 5 he indicates clearly what kind of performance is expected in this profession: *producing sales*. It is also clear from what the sales manager says that a good sales rep is expected to take advice from his boss; something that this sales rep, according to the sales manager, is not doing – for example in segment 5: *you receive what I say but you've not (.) applied what I say*.

This brings us to the second question, that of the relationship between the manager and the sales rep. Underlying everything the sales manager says is the assumption of a hierarchical, authoritarian relationship between himself and his subordinate: that the sales rep is expected to do what his boss tells him, and not challenge him as he does in segment 4: *an' then I talk to you about it an' you tell me that that's not true*. This kind of relationship is of course not unique to this company or particular profession, but is the norm in many businesses and organizations. However, organizations vary in terms of how hierarchical they are, and in terms of the mechanisms available for those 'lower down' to voice their concerns and opinions.

The sales manager's description of the situation indicates that in this profession knowledge and expertise are acquired through practical training on the job. The sales manager tells us that his own expertise was acquired through years of practical experience: *an' I been twenty years in selling(.) advertising an' twelve of that is trade advertising* (segment 4). He clearly sees his role as that of expert, transferring his knowledge to the novice sales rep and guiding him in his work, as reflected in what he says in segment 6:

◎   an' you're willing to receive the instruction an' apply it

◎   I'll be there to work with you, right along side of you

This kind of apprenticeship model of learning is of course common to many professions, particularly in business and trade. But in other professions expert knowledge is acquired, at least initially, through previous training and academic qualifications (for example in medicine and law).

More generally we can say that in this profession performance and success are valued very highly; notice for example the juxtaposition of the verbs *succeed* and *fail* in segment 3. In addition, a job is seen as something that must be 'earned' by producing tangible results. This is expressed quite clearly in the threat at the end of segment 6:

◎ but I've gotta see significant change in the next two weeks ↓or you're not gonna be with this company

Again, this is not to say that performance is not valued in other professions, but it is not always measured via such tangible results as sales figures. And in other professional communities job security may be given more priority than in sales. In fact, the 'hire and fire' mentality evident in this transcript is often considered to be typical of American-style business.

Commentary on Text 7: Teacher (Contrasting text segments) (p. 21)

Paragraphs 2 and 7

◎ The hours were *so* long – I'd get to the office at 6.30am and never leave before 8pm.

◎ But it's more flexible. I can leave school at 4pm and take my work home with me.

Paragraph 3

◎ After leaving school without qualifications and joining the bank aged 16, Emma gave up work in the City at age 24.

◎ After taking her A-levels in evening courses, she enrolled on a full-time BA degree in Education at Middlesex University.

Paragraph 4

◎ Before I went to university, I thought I was the only person who'd done a job for 10 years and hated it,

◎ but when I got to Middlesex I met loads of bankers who'd decided to make a career change as well.

Paragraph 7

◎ I wouldn't say teaching is an easy profession,

◎ In fact I would say it's harder than working in banking.

Paragraph 9

◎ Emma believes the <u>benefits</u> of having her degree

◎ far outweigh the monetary <u>setbacks</u>.

In the examples above, only the repetitions and the sections of text that use clearly contrasting vocabulary have been underlined, but one could argue that other items are also being contrasted, for example in paragraph 4:

◎ done a job for 10 years and hated it

and

◎ decided to make a career change

or the last sentence of paragraphs 2 and 7:

◎ I felt absolutely brain-dead

and

◎ It means I can do something I enjoy and also have a social life

What all the contrasts in the text highlight is how much more personally satisfying the new career is for Emma compared to the old one. Notice the frequent repetitions of the positive verbs of affect *love* and *enjoy* to describe her training and work in education in contrast to the verb *hate* in talking about her work in banking. Work is thus portrayed as a vehicle for personal fulfilment for the individual.

Written workplace genres

In Unit one we looked at some of the differences between everyday language and workplace language. This and the next unit will explore in more detail a number of different types or genres of written and spoken workplace interactions, and examine their structures and characteristics. This unit begins by looking at a range of written genres, and then considers the relationship between written and spoken workplace inter-actions. The focus will be on two opposing but complementary aspects of genres. On the one hand, genres have predictable conventions and structures. But, on the other hand, these conventions are subject to vari-ation and change, which means that genres are also flexible and allow creativity.

Each profession, organization or branch of industry uses its own range of written genres, so it would be impossible to deal with all of them here. However, there are a number of basic written genres, which are used in most organizations. In order to do their work, people need to communi-cate with others inside and outside the organization, and for this letters, **memos**, faxes and email are used. Among the numerous written docu-ments produced, proposals to carry out work and reports about work that has been done are important in many professions and workplaces. In the area of sales, **quotations**, **orders** and **invoices** are central to a smooth exchange of goods. One reason that so many written documents are produced in the workplace is that it is often necessary for future work to have a written record of what has been done previously. It may also be important to have written records for legal reasons, in case there is some dispute about agreements reached or work carried out.

WRITTEN COMMUNICATION: LETTERS, FAX AND EMAIL

The business letter is the traditional mode of written communication in the world of work. But nowadays the fax, and more recently email, have taken over as the most common form of exchanging written messages. The obvious advantage of fax and email is that the exchange of messages is almost instantaneous. However, this does not mean that the business letter has become obsolete. Business letters are still preferred for certain types of correspondence.

In this unit, we are going to look at a series of letters and emails from the world of publishing. The correspondence is between a publisher, Language Publications[1] and a freelance writer, Alison Christy, who is reviewing the pilot edition of a new book, *English the Easy Way*, for the publisher. For textbooks intended to be used for teaching, in particular language teaching, it is common practice first to write a 'pilot edition' which is sent out to independent reviewers (usually teachers) for evaluation and is sometimes tested in actual classrooms. The first part of Text 8: Pilot Edition shows the beginning and end of a letter from the editor, Christine Warner, to the reviewer giving details about the book and instructions for the review. The following three parts show emails sent between the editor's publishing assistant, Martha Westcombe, and the reviewer.

---

1 The names of the publisher, the correspondents and the book are fictional, but the texts themselves are authentic.

Read the four extracts shown in Text 8: Pilot Edition, and answer the following questions:

◎ What similarities and differences do you notice between the letter and the emails? Look in particular at the opening and closing of the messages and the formality of the language.

◎ Are there any differences between the three emails? What do you think is the reason for this?

◎ Why do you think the first text was sent as a letter and the other three as emails? In general, what types of messages do you think are more likely to be sent as letters and what types are more likely to be sent as faxes or emails?

Text 8: Pilot Edition

Letter: From publisher to writer

Dear Alison Christy

ENGLISH THE EASY WAY – PILOT EDITION

Thank you very much for agreeing to review this pilot edition of *English the Easy Way*. This letter provides a short background to the project and a list of points I would like you to consider when you read the units and write your report. I hope that you will enjoy looking at this material.

[. . .]

The deadline for submitting your report is **31 August 2001**. If you feel that you will be unable to meet this deadline, please contact me as soon as possible.

When you receive this package, could you please email Martha Westcombe (mwestcombe@langpubl.co.uk) or telephone her on 0208 462 23 00 to confirm that the materials have arrived safely. Should you have any queries at all about the review or what to include in your report, please do not hesitate to contact me either by telephone or email so that I can clarify anything which is unclear in this letter. Please remember that your comments, both positive and negative, would be appreciated. Do not feel inhibited and rest assured that all the feedback to the authors is anonymized.

I hope that you will enjoy working with this material and I look forward to reading all your feedback.

Very best wishes,

C. Warner

Christine Warner
Editor

Email 1: From publishing assistant to all reviewers

Subject: English the Easy Way Pilot

Dear All,

Many thanks indeed for agreeing to work on this pilot edition of English the Easy Way. I hope you are enjoying the material. I just wanted to check that you have all the information you require, Please let me know if you are going to have trouble making the 31 August deadline. I look forward to reading your feedback.

Please don't hesitate to contact me if you have any questions.

Very best wishes,

Yours sincerely,

Martha Westcombe
Publishing Assistant

Email 2: From reviewer to publishing assistant

Dear Martha,

Yes, I received all the material, and don't think I should have any trouble making the 31 August deadline. Will I be able to reach you in August in case I have any questions?

Best wishes,
Alison

Email 3: From publishing assistant to reviewer

Dear Alison,

Thank you for your reply.

Yes, Christine or myself will be available if you have any questions.

Martha

Check your answers at the end of this unit (pp. 48–9), and then read the commentary below.

Commentary

The main difference between the letter and the emails which you probably noticed is the style: the letter is more formal than the emails. There are a number of reasons for this. First of all, the letter represents the actual job assignment, giving details of what the reviewer is expected to do, the due date and contact details; therefore it makes sense that the style should be fairly formal. The emails are less important types of document: they are simply communications exchanged about the job assignment that has already been sent and received.

Another reason, according to Louhiala-Salminen (1999) is that whereas the conventions of business letters are well-established, those of fax, and in particular email, are not as stabilized. Therefore one finds more variation in the language used in faxes and emails, because writers are less constrained to conform to certain standards. Notice for example how the first email has two closing salutations (*Very best wishes* and *Yours sincerely*), whereas the last one has none. Perhaps because of this lack of standardization, the style of business emails seems to be influenced by that of personal emails, which use many features of spoken language, for example contractions (*don't*).

A further reason for the informality of fax and email given by Louhiala-Salminen is the **context** dependence of these types of messages. Faxes and emails are often less explicit than letters and assume the reader already has some background knowledge about the situation. This is also the case for the emails we have looked at; for example the reader of the last email knows that *if you have any questions* refers to questions about the book review. The notion of context dependency is closely linked to that of **intertextuality**, which refers to how texts are linked to one another. Thus emails often refer back to earlier letters and emails, and do not repeat information that was already mentioned in previous correspondence. In our examples, all four texts have intertextual links. In the first email, *the material* refers to the pilot edition of the book the reviewer has received, and *the information* makes reference to information sent in the letter. The second email (written by the reviewer) again mentions *the material* which presumably refers both to the book and the letter received, and both the first and second email make reference to *the 31 August deadline* first mentioned in the letter. Notice how the definite article *the* is used in the emails to refer to items that have been mentioned or background knowledge that is assumed to be shared. Because of the assumed **shared knowledge** and the intertextual links, the three emails become progressively shorter and less explicit. Responses to emails often include the original message, which makes it easy for the respondee to refer implicitly to items mentioned in the original message.

The reason why the first message was sent as a letter and the other three as emails has already been referred to above: the letter constitutes the job assignment, and is therefore a more important document than the emails. In general, we can say that for documents which are important and have some kind of legal status, sending them via the usual postal system with or in the form of a business letter is still the preferred method. Where speed is of the essence, but having a written record is less important, it seems faxes and emails are preferred. As technology evolves, this is something that may change with time; for example it is already possible to send documents as email attachments.

The characteristics of business letters, faxes and emails give us an interesting insight into how genres evolve to meet the changing demands of the discourse community. Whereas business letters represent a stable genre with well-established structural and stylistic conventions, faxes and especially email are still evolving and thus subject to more variation and instability.

SALES PROMOTION LETTERS

Thus far we have looked at written communication between people working together (although not within the same organization). But a great number of texts written in the workplace are aimed at potential customers and users of a product or service outside the organization. In this section we will look at sales promotion letters, which have the purpose of persuading prospective customers to buy a product or service.

Remember that in Unit one a genre was said to be defined primarily by its communicative goal or purpose. According to Swales (1990), written genres are structured in terms of separate 'moves', each serving a particular communicative purpose relative to the overall goal of the genre. As Bhatia (1993: 45) points out, the main function of a sales promotion letter is persuasive: it attempts to elicit a particular response from the reader, i.e. to get them to buy the product or service. As sales promotion letters are usually unsolicited, they must capture the attention of the potential customer. In order to do this, such letters tend to include the following moves (Bhatia, 1993: 46–9):

1   establishing credentials

2   introducing the offer

    i)   offering the product or service

    ii)   essential detailing of the offer

    iii) indicating value of the offer

3   offering incentives

4   enclosing documents

5   soliciting response

6   using pressure tactics

7   ending politely

In the first move, 'establishing credentials', the writer shows knowledge of the potential needs of the customer and indicates how his/her organization is able to fulfil them. Move 2, 'introducing the offer', involves presenting the goods or services offered. As this is the most important part of letter, it is usually made up of three sub-moves or 'steps', as shown above. The first step simply makes the offer, the second describes it in detail and the third step evaluates the offer in terms of how it will benefit the customer. Move 3, 'offering incentives' is a further strategy used to persuade the customer, for example by offering discounts or a making a special offer. Move 4, 'enclosing documents' is used when other documents, for example brochures, are sent with the letter. This is a useful strategy to keep the actual letter short, but still provide the potential customer with all the relevant information. The move 'soliciting response' encourages the receiver of the letter to get in contact with the writer. 'Using pressure tactics' is similar to 'offering incentives', but it usually occurs at the end of the letter, and often refers to some kind of deadline or limit to the offer.

Activity

Read Text 9: Printer's Letter, which is a sales promotion letter from a British printer aimed at companies who might need their services for labels, stationery or other products:

◎ Which of the above moves are used in the letter?

◎ Where does each move begin and end? (Note that a move does not necessarily correspond to a paragraph.)

◎ Based on your analysis of the letter, which moves would you say always occur in a sales promotion letter, i.e. are obligatory, and which are optional?

Text 9: Printer's Letter

Dear Sirs

As a well-established business, we are only too aware of the importance of maintaining a high profile in today's competitive market. From our experience as lithographic printers and label manufacturers, we understand the need for high quality work to identify and promote one's products and we realize that the printed image can be as important as the product itself.

The services we offer are unique, having lithographic and flexographic printing facilities in house. Our recent investment in a new 6 colour flexographic printing press, with in-line foil blocking, U.V. varnishing, die cutting and sheet finishing facilities, gives us the capability of producing multi-coloured labels on a variety of self-adhesive substrates. This press has the added ability to produce wet strength labels on unsupported label papers, generally considered to be the domain of the lithographic process.

We offer a fully computerized design service with one of the most innovative designers within this industry. This eliminates the need for expensive third party design houses, which can sometimes lack the finite technical knowledge off the various printing processes.

If you are currently considering re-designing your labels or stationery, we would welcome the opportunity of submitting a quotation for any of your company's printing requirements, or we would be happy to discuss and try to solve any problems you may be experiencing.

We will contact you shortly to discuss in more detail, the products and services on offer to you and answer any questions you may have, but if we can be of any assistance in the meantime, please do not hesitate to contact us.

Yours faithfully

G. Turner

Gary Turner
Sales Manager

Check your answers at the end of this unit (p. 50), and then read the following commentary.

Commentary

This printer's sales promotion letter uses only the obligatory and none of the optional moves. The writer establishes the company's credentials by emphasizing their expertise and experience:

◎　　As a well-established business

◎　　From our experience as lithographic printers and label manufacturers

and by showing their understanding of the customer's needs:

◎　　we are only too aware of

◎　　the need for

◎　　we realize that

Introducing the offer, the most important move, takes up most of the letter. Step 3, indicating value of the offer, is particularly long and spans two paragraphs. The fourth paragraph shows how the offer can benefit the customer in a particular situation: if they need to redesign their labels or stationery.

The last two moves, soliciting response and ending politely, are merged into one here, which is not unusual for letters like this. Soliciting response is a very important move, as further contact between the company and the potential customer is the pre-condition for fulfilling the purpose of the letter: to win new customers. In this letter, the writer not only solicits a response (*please do not hesitate to contact us*), but announces that he or someone from the company will initiate further communication (*We will contact you shortly . . .*).

FLEXIBILITY AND VARIATION IN GENRE

The previous example, Text 9: Printer's Letter, follows a standard move structure for this genre. But this does not mean that sales promotion letters always follow this schema exactly. Some of the moves may occur in a different order, and there may also be variations from culture to culture or from business to business in how letters like this are written.

Text 10: Advertiser's Letter shows a sales promotion letter from a North American company which specializes in designing postcard advertising for customers selling equipment to professionals, for example dental supplies. Read it and answer the following questions:

◎   Which moves are used in the letter and in which order do they occur?

◎   Where does each move begin and end?

◎   In what way is the letter different from the printer's letter? Look at the move structure, the layout and the style of the letter.

Text 10: Advertiser's Letter

A Proven Formula . . .

GUARANTEED to Generate New Business

Dear Marketer:

If I can give you:

   –   a quick, easy, hassle-free way to generate new business,
   –   a steady stream of pre-qualified sales leads,
   –   and I'm willing to guarantee the results,

would you be willing to discuss it with me?

We've been in business for ten years, serving seven different markets. Over 1,200 active clients currently use our direct response programs each year to generate new business. The formula for their success, tried and proven over the past ten years, is so certain that we even guarantee the results.

Our formula for success, based on our extensive experience, is very simple:

   Offer: We work with clients to design an offer especially for our medium that compels response in our marketplace.

Message: We build a message and card design around that offer that is informative and catches attention, and that we know speaks to the market.

Audience: We carefully select and refine our lists to reach true, authorized buyers covering the maximum purchasing power in the marketplace.

Timing: Extra attention is paid to ensure the proper mailing dates in order to coincide with key buying times (and the times you need to support your major trade show investments)

Guarantee: We minimize your risk by **GUARANTEEING** the response.

The bottom line is a *risk-free* opportunity to put your sales message in front of the entire market of ready-to-buy prospects . . . and to create a steady stream of qualified, closeable sales leads that convert to sales.

Please give me a call at 800–862–6630 for more details or return this fax today.

Sincerely,

C. Chmela

Chris Chmela
President

Check your answers at the end of this unit (pp. 50–1), and then read the commentary below.

Commentary

Text 10: Advertiser's Letter differs in a number of ways from Text 9: Printer's Letter. For example, it does not begin by establishing the firm's credentials, but starts with a question addressed to the reader:

If I can give you . . . would you be willing to discuss it with me?

As part of this question, the services offered by the company are presented, laid out as three separate bullet points:

- a quick, easy, hassle-free way to generate new business,

- a steady stream of pre-qualified sales leads,

- and I'm willing to guarantee the results,

We can therefore describe this opening as Step 1 of Move 2: offering the product or service.

The next paragraph constitutes a standard Move 1, establishing credentials, where the company refers to the extent of their experience and the number of clients they have:

◎   We've been in the business for ten years

◎   serving seven different markets

◎   Over 1,200 active clients

as well as to how they satisfy their clients' needs:

◎   we even guarantee the results.

So the advertiser's letter varies the standard move structure, with the first step of Move 2 coming before Move 1. Bhatia says that Move 1 and 2 are in fact frequently reversed in sales promotion letters.

Next, the services are described in detail, so this constitutes Step 2 of Move 2: essential detailing of offer. The reader's attention is drawn to each of the services offered through the use of a key word in bold before each description:

Offer

Message

Audience

Timing

Guarantee

This contrasts with Move 2, Step 2 of the printer's letter, where the services are described in a standard paragraph of unbroken prose.

The two letters end in a similar fashion, with Step 3 of Move 2, indicating value of the offer, followed by Moves 5 and 6, soliciting response and ending politely. The advertiser's letter evaluates the offer as *a risk-free opportunity*, and provides two options for responding to the letter, by phoning or sending a fax.

Note that in both letters positive evaluation of the offer is not limited to Move 2, Step 3, but is in fact spread throughout the letter, particularly in the other parts of Move 2. Thus in the printer's letter the services are introduced as *unique* in Step 1, and in the advertiser's letter each of the services described in Step 2 is also evaluated positively, 'a message . . . *that we know speaks to the market*'.

What is most striking about this letter in contrast to the printer's letter is the non-standard layout and the direct language. It is not written in continuous prose, but is broken up into lists and bullet points, and uses bold layout and capitalization to highlight particular words. The writer gets straight to the point with the direct question at the beginning, and the offer is quite strongly expressed, using words such as *proven, guarantee, bottom-line, risk-free*. It is also less formal, in particular in the initial question, where the writer uses *I* and *me*, instead of *we*, and the colloquial expression *hassle-free*.

All these features of the letter have the purpose of capturing the attention of the reader, and this is of course designed to serve the overall purpose of the genre – to persuade the reader to 'buy'. Does this mean that this letter is therefore a better sales promotion letter than the previous one? The answer is that it depends on the cultural context, as the differences we observe between these two letters may be due to national and/or business culture. Bhatia notes that Move 3, offering incentives, is particularly common in Singapore and other countries in the East. Neither of the letters we have looked at, both from Western countries, have this move. But the features of the advertiser's letter identified above seem more typical of a North American than a British style of writing. In British culture, such a letter could be considered 'over the top', and might therefore not be successful. The differences may also have something to do with the type of business: advertising is typically associated with more 'hype', whereas this may not be considered appropriate in the printing industry. However, we would need more examples of sales promotion letters from each type of business to be sure.

WRITTEN AND SPOKEN GENRES AT WORK

In this book, written and spoken workplace genres are dealt with in separate units. But just as different written texts may be linked to one another, as we saw in the example above of the letter and emails between the publisher and the reviewer, so written texts may have intertextual links with spoken genres. For example, in addition to corresponding by letter and email, the publisher and the reviewer might also have spoken to each other about the same job on the telephone. A particular work procedure might involve a whole series of written and spoken genres. A good example of this is a business meeting, which is preceded by the distribution of a written agenda for the meeting to the participants (see Unit one), and is followed up by the distribution of written minutes of the meeting.

Activity

Look at the two texts below from the same American company as the promotional letter above. This company employs a sales force who sell over the telephone and are monitored and trained by a sales manager. The first, Text 11: Conversation Stoppers, is a draft document drawn up by the sales manager to use in training his sales force: it contains some information about 'conversation stoppers', i.e. things the sales reps should *not* say to begin their conversations with prospective customers. The sales manager gave this draft document to his boss, the president of the company, who scribbled some handwritten notes on it. The second text, Text 12: Talking about 'Conversation Stoppers', is a transcript of part of a conversation in which the sales manager, Joe, and the president, Chris, discussed this document, and Chris made some suggestions how it could be improved.

◎   Compare the two texts.

◎   Can you identify the parts of the conversation in which Chris refers to the handwritten notes he has made on Joe's draft?

Text 11: Conversation Stoppers

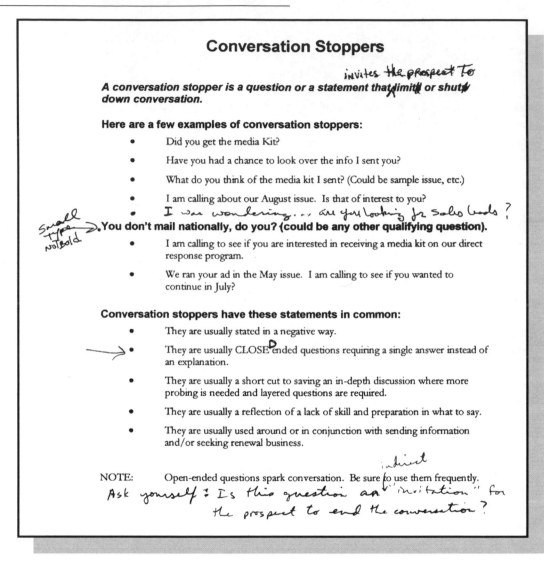

Conversation Stoppers

invites the prospect To [handwritten]

A conversation stopper is a question or a statement that ~~limits~~ or ~~shuts~~ down conversation.

Here are a few examples of conversation stoppers:

- Did you get the media Kit?

- Have you had a chance to look over the info I sent you?

- What do you think of the media kit I sent? (Could be sample issue, etc.)

- I am calling about our August issue. Is that of interest to you?

- *I was wondering... are you looking for Sales leads?* [handwritten]

small type not bold [handwritten margin note] → **.You don't mail nationally, do you? (could be any other qualifying question).**

- I am calling to see if you are interested in receiving a media kit on our direct response program.

- We ran your ad in the May issue. I am calling to see if you wanted to continue in July?

Conversation stoppers have these statements in common:

- They are usually stated in a negative way.

→ - They are usually CLOSED ended questions requiring a single answer instead of an explanation.

- They are usually a short cut to saving an in-depth discussion where more probing is needed and layered questions are required.

- They are usually a reflection of a lack of skill and preparation in what to say.

- They are usually used around or in conjunction with sending information and/or seeking renewal business.

NOTE: Open-ended questions spark conversation. Be sure to use them frequently. *indirect* [handwritten above]

Ask yourself: Is this question an "invitation" for the prospect to end the conversation? [handwritten]

Text 12: Talking about 'Conversation Stoppers'

1	Chris	uh (.) I got a suggestion (.) by the way with this
2	Joe	okay
3	Chris	two things. uh (.) I don't know why this is (.) large. isn't this the same as all the rest of these? it's just another (.) example?
4	Joe	yeah it should be (1.5) yeah that's just another example
5	Chris	⌊I was thinking this also (.) the 'I was wondering' approach? hehehehehehehehehe
6	Joe	⌊yeah I was wondering heh yeah I like that okay
7	Chris	uhm (.) an' a– an' maybe just a note at the end here that says to the person ↑ ask yourself is this question (.) a an indirect invitation for the prospect to end the conversation ⌊Joe: yeah⌋ because (.) I mean if they really answered that honestly almost all of these are
8	Joe	yeah that's right
9	Chris	so an' you *might* include– what I had here was some conversation *star*ters or approa– you know
10	Joe	.hh okay I hadn't even *thought* about that yet but good I'm glad you have a (.) ↓ a note on that
11	Chris	okay
12	Joe	'cause I wanna (.) ↑ an' I'm– this is *partially* what I had col*lec*ted an' I wanna get (.) what I *can*, an' then (.) kind o' have a little workshop on it an' get some feedback to where we're going with it an' (.) what uh (.)
13	Chris	okay
14	Joe	an' then an ongoing list ↓ like you said ⌊Chris: yeah⌋ we'll just keep a note of 'em
15	Chris	⌊they gotta be (.) they *got*ta be involved in it it won't– it won't work as a lecture
16	Joe	no I'm not trying to do it as a lecture ↑ my *prob*lem though is that they're not I'm not getting a lot of *feed*back from them an' it's like pulling *teeth* to get them to (.) to (.) /ad*mit*/
17	Chris	⌊well *yeah* because they're em*bar*rassed about it
18	Joe	*yeah*! heheheh so (.)
19	Chris	⌊heheheh
20	Chris	but– but you know you can– after you've presented this to 'em you can *al*ways listen to the conversations an'– an' say ↑ here's that conversation starter it's right here on the *list* ↓ conversation stopper yeah ↑ it's right here on the *list*

21	Joe	yeah)
22	Chris	⌊and you wonder why that conversation went nowhere here's why
23	Joe	an' that– uh– that's excellent an' I've got uh– ↑ some of these are because I listened to them, some of 'em are their input ↓ so it's (.) it's a com– combination of both

Check your answers at the end of this unit (pp. 51–2), before you read the commentary on the two texts below.

Commentary

The conversation between Joe and Chris is *about* a written document, which means their talk would not actually make any sense if we did not have access to the list of 'conversation stoppers'. This is quite typical of many workplace conversations, where speakers may be discussing some written document they have in front of them or something they are looking at on a computer screen. But the conversation is linked not only to the written document it is about, but also to other types of interactions in the company, as we learn from what Chris and Joe say.

Activity

Look again at the conversation between Chris and Joe, and make a list of all spoken and written communication within the company that is referred or alluded to.

Check your answers at the end of this unit (p. 52), before you read the commentary on the two texts below.

Commentary

The conversation between Chris and Joe is simply permeated with intertextual links. Not only is the whole conversation about a specific written document, but it is also full of references to other spoken and written texts: to future versions of the document they are discussing, as well as to various types of verbal interactions between Joe and members of his sales team. What this illustrates is that texts produced in the workplace cannot be understood in isolation, divorced from their context. They must be seen as part a whole work-related process, each text playing a particular role within that process. In fact Devitt (1991) says that the interactions among texts within a profession create a kind of 'macrotext', which in a sense defines the discourse community.

SUMMARY

This unit has examined written texts used in the workplace for communication between people working together in the same profession, between businesses and their customers, and between co-workers within the same organization. The emphasis has been on the following characteristics of written genres.

◎   Genres have predictable conventions and structures, but they are also subject to variation and change.

◎   Written genres can be analysed in terms of a 'move' structure, each move serving a particular communicative purpose which is part of the overall goal of the genre.

◎   Written texts in the workplace are linked to other texts, including spoken ones, through intertextuality, and thereby form part of a larger work process.

Extension

In this unit, we have only been able to examine a limited range of workplace texts and contexts. But you can use the ideas explored in this unit to investigate other texts from other areas of work. Depending on the type of access you have to texts produced at work, perhaps through your own work experience, or that of friends or family, or through written material you receive through the post, do one or both of the following activities:

1   Collect several examples of the same type of text, for example promotional leaflets, emails, quotes, invoices, memos, training manuals. Decide what you think the purpose of each genre is and try to devise a move structure. Do you notice any differences between the various

47

texts of the same genre you have collected? How might you explain these differences? Are they just different ways of achieving the same goal, or could they be due to differences in profession, culture, intended readership?

2   Collect a number of texts from the same place of work. Identify all the intertextual links between these texts, for example repeated vocabulary or phrases, or references to the same processes or people. What have you learned about this place of work from the texts, for example about the work itself or the way people work together and communicate?

ANSWERS TO THE ACTIVITIES

Answers for Text 8: Pilot Edition (pp. 31–3)

Business letters have certain well-established conventions, as you can see in this example: they start with a salutation (*Dear . . .*), which is followed by a subject line in bold before the main body of the letter. It is usual to start the letter with some sort of reference to previous contact, here thanking the addressee for agreeing to review the book. The end of the letter also follows established conventions: there is a closing line which refers to further contact using the standard phrase *I look forward to . . .*, and a closing salutation (*Very best wishes*), followed by the signature, name and position of the writer. The emails also use some of these conventions in the opening and closing salutations:

◎   Dear . . .

◎   (Very) best wishes

◎   Yours sincerely

The subject line does not appear after the opening salutation, but at the top of the message, and of course it is the first thing the receiver sees when the email arrives in his or her inbox.

The three emails also differ from one another. The first one, addressed to all the reviewers, is markedly more formal and longer than the last two, which are between one of the reviewers and the publishing assistant. The first email is the most 'letter-like' of the three, using standard polite openings and closings:

◎ Many thanks

◎ I look forward to

It also has the most formal closing salutation with two separate formulae:

◎ Very best wishes

◎ Yours sincerely

The second email only uses a friendly and less formal *best wishes*, whereas the last email has no closing salutation at all.

The biggest difference, between the letter and the emails, apart from the obvious difference in length, is that the emails are more informal. Whereas the letter uses the addressee's and the sender's full name, most of the emails use only first names. While the letter is opened and closed using standard formulae, the emails get to the point much more quickly and dispense with many of the standard phrases typical for letters. Even the first email, which is most letter-like of the three, uses less formal language than the letter. Compare the opening and closing lines:

◎ **Opening letter:**

Thank you very much for agreeing to review . . .

◎ **Opening email 1:**

Many thanks indeed for agreeing to work on . . .

◎ **Closing letter:**

I hope that you will enjoy working with this material and look forward to reading all your feedback.

◎ **Closing email 1:**

Please don't hesitate to contact me if you have any questions.

Notice that the writers of the emails use contractions (e.g. *don't*), whereas this is avoided in the letter. Compare the two very similar lines in the letter and the first email:

◎ **Letter:**

Should you have any queries at all about the review or what to include in your report, please *do not* hesitate to contact me . . .

◎ **Email 1:**

Please *don't* hesitate to contact me if you have any questions.

Answers for Text 9: Printer's Letter (p. 37)

◎ **Move 1** – Establishing credentials:

> As a well-established business . . . we realize that the printed image can be as important as the product itself.

◎ **Move 2** – Introducing the offer:

(i) Offering the product or service:
> The services we offer are unique, having lithographic and flexographic printing facilities in house.

(ii) Essential detailing of the offer:
> Our recent investment in a new 6 colour flexographic printing press . . . generally considered to be the domain of the lithographic process.

(iii) Indicating value of the offer:
> We offer a fully computerized design service . . . or we would be happy to discuss and try to solve any problems you may be experiencing.

◎ **Moves 5 and 6** – Soliciting response and ending politely:

> We will contact you shortly . . . but if we can be of any assistance in the meantime, please do not hesitate to contact us.

Obligatory moves: establishing credentials, introducing the offer, soliciting response, ending politely.

Optional moves: offering incentives, enclosing documents, using pressure tactics (these do not occur).

Answers for Text 10: Advertiser's Letter (pp. 39–40)

The moves occur in the following order:

◎ **Move 2** – Introducing the offer, **Step 1** – Offering the product or service:

> If I can give you . . .
> would you be willing to discuss it with me?

◎ **Move 1** – Establishing credentials:

> We've been in the business for ten years, serving seven different markets . . . that we even guarantee the results.

⊚ **Move 2, Step 2** – Essential detailing of the offer:

> Our formula for success, based on our extensive experience, is very simple:
>
> . . .
>
> **Guarantee**: We minimize your risk by GUARANTEEING the response.

⊚ **Move 2, Step 3** – Indicating value of the offer:

> The bottom line is a risk-free opportunity . . . and to create a steady stream of qualified, closeable sales leads that convert to sales.

⊚ **Moves 5 and 6** – Soliciting response and ending politely:

> Please give me a call at 800 . . . for more details or return this fax today.

Answers for Text 11: Conversation Stoppers and Text 12: Talking about 'Conversation Stoppers' (pp. 44–6)

References to handwritten notes

In the following parts of the conversation Chris refers to the handwritten notes he has made on Joe's draft:

⊚ **Turn 3**: *I don't know why this is (.) large. isn't this the same as all the rest of these?*

This refers to the note in the left margin of the written document: *small type not bold*. He is pointing out that Joe has made a mistake by making this line (*You don't mail nationally do you . . .*) look like a heading, when it is simply another item in the list of 'conversation stoppers'.

⊚ **Turn 5**: *also (.) th: 'I was wondering' approach?*

This refers to the handwritten bullet point Chris has added at the end of the first list of bullet points: *I was wondering . . . are you looking for sales leads?* He is proposing that *I was wondering . . .* is also a 'conversation stopper' – a bad way to begin a sales conversation.

⊚ **Turn 7**: *uhm (.) an' a– an' maybe just a note at the end here, that says to the person ↑ ask yourself is this question (.) a an indirect invitation for the prospect to end the conversation.*

51

Here Chris is clearly talking about the note at the bottom of the page, which has nearly the same wording: *Ask yourself. Is this question an indirect 'invitation' for the prospect to end the conversation?*

References to other communication

The following written and spoken communication is referred to in the conversation between Chris and Joe:

◎ **Turn 9**: *an' you might include . . . some conversation starters.*

Chris refers to some model ways of beginning a sales conversation ('conversation starters') which he has jotted down and proposes Joe include in the document he intends to give the sales reps.

◎ **Turn 14**: *an ongoing list (.) we'll just keep a note of 'em.*

Apparently, Joe intends to add to his list of 'conversation stoppers', as he gets more feedback from the sales reps.

◎ **Turn 12** (Joe): *have a little workshop on it.*

Turn 15 (Chris): *it won't work as a lecture.*

Here Joe and Chris refer to a training session Joe intends to run for his sales team on this topic.

◎ **Turn 16** (Joe): *I'm not getting a lot of feedback from them.*

Turn 20 (Chris): *an' say here's that conversation starter it's right here on the list.*

Turn 23 (Joe): *some of 'em are their input.*

These comments seem to refer to individual conversations between Joe and members of his sales team, although they could also be about workshops with the whole sales force.

◎ **Turn 20** (Chris): *you can always listen to their conversations.*

Turn 23 (Joe): *some of these are because I listened to them.*

Here the speakers allude to the fact that Joe listens in on conversations between sales reps and customers. This involves an interesting mode of one-way communication, with the sales manager in the role of overhearer.

Spoken workplace genres

The last unit focused mainly on written workplace genres, and in this unit we now turn to spoken genres. Some spoken workplace genres, such as meetings, for example, are very structured and follow a pre-set agenda. Others, for example many negotiations, may be planned in advance, but may actually develop quite differently from the original plan. Still others are not planned at all, and arise spontaneously out of a particular situation. Throughout this unit we will be looking at how the work situation and the roles of the speakers affect the interactions.

MEETINGS

Meetings play an important role in almost every organization, and a great deal of working time is spent in meetings. As meetings tend to involve multi-party talk – that is talk between three or more people, it is usually necessary to have a person who organizes the meeting and leads the discussion. This person is known as the 'chair', and is often a more senior person in the company, for example a head of department.

Activity

Text 13: Management Meeting shows the beginning of a management meeting that took place in a small North American company.

The participants are:

◎ Tom, who is the CEO (chief executive officer) and head of the company;

◎ Mike, the president, who is responsible for the running of the company;

◎ Amy, the chief financial officer (the financial manager);

◎ Bill, the sales manager.

Mike is chairing the meeting. One of the main topics to be discussed is the fact that one of the sales reps (David Johnson) is leaving and that a new person (Jim Murray) will take over some selling for the company on a contract basis (but will be based in another city).

This activity looks more closely at the role played and the language used by the chair of a meeting. First read through the transcript and answer the following questions:

◎ What does this initial part of the meeting tell you about the role of the chair?

◎ What is Mike, the chair, doing in this part of the meeting?

Text 13: Management Meeting

1	Mike	okay (.) the uh topics I wanted to handle when we get together right now were (.) uhm distribution of David Johnson's database[1] after he's gone and that's something we have to decide kind of now. and uh and that relates to the fact that Jim Murray is uh (.) likely gonna start working with us within the week. uh he'd like to– by the way he'd like to start working with us right away if he can without coming up first, and so we gotta talk about that a little bit too

1 The 'database' refers to all the customers and potential customers a sales rep deals with.

2	Amy	well we have to have signed agreement before (.) we give him anything
3	Mike	⌊yeah
4	Mike	yeah but I mean that can be done by fax (3) uhm (.)
5	Amy	what's the downside of having him start before (.) really isn't one is there?
6	Mike	↑well the only downside is that we ha– then we have to have a written agreement before we actually *ever* meet him face to face
	(2)	
7	Tom	we've met him face to face
8	Mike	well in a totally different context though ⌊Tom: (Mm)⌋ uhm so anyway that's– *one* thing is what to do about David Johnson's database, the second thing is (.) uh consolidated sales force idea that (.) Bill would like to propose, and uh potential F.G. Deck[2] circulation changes which we don't necessarily have to do right now but we do have on our schedule for getting the ninety-eight planning by Friday uhm certain things. and part of that has to do with what happens with F.G. and the other thing is what we do about with N.T. Deck, because there are also some other ideas on the table for that. so uh (.) I think the first thing we should deal with is– is uh (.) is the first two
9	Amy	okay
10	Mike	and hopefully we'll get to the other ones
11	Mike	so uhm (.) David Johnson's database – here's the deal. with– with Murray um what we offered him was basically [. . .]

Commentary

Text 13: Management Meeting shows that the chair basically controls the meeting: he opens and closes it and introduces the topics to be handled. In this initial part of the meeting, Mike gives an overview of what the meeting will be about and goes over the topics to be discussed. Usually the

---

2 'F.G. Deck' and 'N.T. Deck' refer to advertising products the company sells.

participants in a meeting will have received a written agenda beforehand with a list of these topics (often they have a chance to suggest topics before the meeting).

Mike uses metalanguage (language about language) to refer to the topics which will be discussed during the meeting. Words and phrases like *discussed* or *give an overview* in the previous sentences are metalinguistic. He also uses discourse-organizing words and expressions to structure the overview he gives and link the main points. For example, by using *by the way* in Turn 1, he shows that this point is a subsidiary one related to the previous point.

Activity

Look at Text 13: Management Meeting again and make a note of the following:

◎   metalanguage used by Mike to refer to topics to be discussed;

◎   discourse-organizing language that helps Mike structure his overview of the meeting.

(See the commentary at the end of this unit, p. 71.)

As the text and activities above show, meetings (at least well-organized ones) are very structured interactions. They have clear beginnings, middles and ends, with the chair playing an important role in structuring the meeting. A good chair should make sure that all the topics on the agenda are covered and that the participants do not deviate too much from the main points to be discussed. The other types of workplace interactions we will look at in this unit are not as tightly structured and controlled as meetings, but they nevertheless have identifiable structures.

NEGOTIATING

Many aspects of work and business communication involve negotiating. A negotiation is basically about trying to reach a mutually satisfactory agreement in a situation where two people or parties have some differing (but also some shared) interests and goals. Sales negotiations, in which buyers and sellers discuss the price and other conditions for the purchase of a product or service, are usually carefully prepared and may last hours or even days. But negotiating can involve all kinds of things, for example trying to get a rise from your boss; and, as we'll see in the example below, negotiations can also occur quite spontaneously.

A great deal has been written about the structure of negotiations and the skills a good negotiator should have. Most negotiations go through the following four phases:

1   exchanging information;

2   bidding;

3   bargaining;

4   settling and concluding.

Exchanging information is essential before beginning a negotiation, so that both parties know what the interests and needs of the other side are. Bidding marks the beginning of the actual negotiation, and involves making initial offers or proposals. Bargaining is the core phase of the negotiation, and here the negotiators argue their case, try to persuade the other party and may link their offers to certain conditions. A successful negotiation ends in a mutually satisfactory agreement in the settling and concluding phase.

Activity

Text 14: Negotiating about Applications shows a negotiation which occurred spontaneously between two colleagues, Don and Andy, who work in a departmental office of a North American university. Andy is Don's superior. They are discussing student applications to the department, and how often the incoming applications should be checked and the information entered into the office computer system. Although neither of the speakers has prepared this negotiation, it still goes through the four phases identified above: (1) information exchange; (2) bidding; (3) bargaining; and (4) settling and concluding.

Read Text 14: Negotiating about Applications, then do the following:

◎ Divide the conversation into the four phases of a negotiation.

◎ Make a note of any clues in the text that helped you to decide where each phase begins and ends. Clues could be: the content of the conversation; the words speakers use; their intonation (whether speakers raise or lower their voices); and non-linguistic information, such as pauses (see Notes on transcription, p. xi).

Text 14: Negotiating about Applications

1	Andy	did you check all these people out next door?[3]
2	Don	ah yes
3	Andy	okay
4	Don	as of (.) this day
5	Andy	↑oh ↓aha
6	Don	so I can do 'em (.) let's say weekly ↓or something like that from here on out ↓I don't think it pays to do it any more often than that
7	Andy	↑well weekly, I mean you have to do it . . . (1.5) ah (.) more often than that right now for this week an' next week 'cause we gotta– (.) have 'em all entered into the system by a week on Friday (1) so– any ones that are complete a–
8	Don	⌊↑yeah. ↓but we're only talking about (.) a comparatively small number of *stray* (.) ⌊Andy: Yeah⌋ individual stray fo– ↑you know you know you don't even *en*ter ↓the individual letters an'– and transcripts do you?
9	Andy	ah (.) *no*, but we wan'– but–
10	Don	so?
11	Andy	I'm holding off entering these– *this* week ↓until they're complete
	(3)	
12	Don	well then we'll check 'em at the end of this week or at the beginning of *next* week, that's what I'm *say*ing

---

3 The phrase 'these people next door' refers to the applications which are kept in the room next door, not to actual people.

13	Andy	I might check 'em tomorrow or something just to–
14	Don	okay
15	Andy	just to have more–
16	Don	⌊whatever you *want* but I– I honestly don't even think it's worth it
17	Andy	yeah
18	Don	I don't think you're gonna (.) come up with enough to make it worth– the ti–
19	Andy	⌊↓yeah /??/
	(1)	
20	Andy	right
21	Don	[voice changes] on the other hand it doesn't really take *that long.* it takes about fifteen minutes
22	Andy	⌊yeah it's–
23	Don	to go through the whole box
24	Andy	⌊alright yeah
25	Don	it's not that big a deal. you want me to do it? I'll be happy to do it
26	Andy	no don't (1) ↑ you know– lemme– *I'm* gonna do it ↓I'm looking for something to *do* honestly so–
27	Andy	[takes the box with the applications] I'll take that
28	Don	↑I don't know *why* (.) we don't start entering them like they are
29	Andy	'cause I don't want to have to go into– all of 'em twice and (.) I have all the complete over here and once I enter 'em I put 'em over here. (1) and we'd have to look *here* and look *there* I mean–
30	Don	okay
31	Andy	[Is moving away] /??????/
32	Don	you're the boss
		[Andy leaves the room]

Check your answers at the end of this unit (p. 72), then read the commentary below.

Commentary

The most important type of clue to the phases of the negotiation is the actual content of what the two speakers are saying. So the conversation actually starts off as an exchange of information, until Don makes a suggestion (*So I can do 'em*) which can be classified as a 'bid' and marks the beginning of the negotiation. The bargaining phase, which involves arguing about how often the applications should be checked, makes up the most important part of the conversation. In the settling and concluding phase Don then agrees to check the applications more often than once a week.

But there are other types of clues as well. Intonation and pauses can be important in signalling conversational structure. Speakers often drop their voice at the end of one phase of talk and then raise their voice at the beginning of a new phase, and they sometimes pause between phases. So at the end of the information exchange phase (Turn 5) Andy drops his voice, and at the end of Turn 6 Don's voice drops to signal the end of his 'bid'. There is a one-minute pause after Turn 19, before Don first initiates the settling and concluding phase in Turn 21, and his voice goes up again when he re-opens the bargaining phase in Turn 28.

Speakers also sometimes use **discourse markers** to initiate new phases in the conversation. These are words like *and, so, but, then* which show how different parts of the discourse relate to one another. By beginning with the discourse marker *so* in Turn 6 (*so I can do 'em*), Don shows that his suggestion is based on the information exchange that has just taken place. Don also uses the discourse marker *on the other hand* to initiate the settling and concluding phase in Turn 21. This discourse marker introduces a conciliatory note, as it shows that Don can also see Andy's point of view. The fact that his tone of voice changes also indicates a change in direction within the conversation.

SPEAKERS' ROLES

The following activity examines the way in which workplace roles can affect the development and outcome of interactions.

The aim of a negotiation, as stated at the beginning of this section, is to arrive at a mutually satisfactory agreement. Look through Text 14: Negotiating about Applications again and answer the following questions:

◎   Do you think the agreement reached in this particular negotiation is satisfactory for both parties?

◎   How do you think the relationship between the speakers and their respective roles in the organization might have affected the outcome?

Although in the end Don agrees to do things Andy's way, he does not really seem convinced that this is the best solution. This is indicated, on the one hand, by the fact that he re-opens the negotiation after first having agreed to Andy's preferred course of action. His tongue-in-cheek remark, *you're the boss*, at the end (Turn 32) indicates that he is not really convinced, but is merely agreeing with Andy because of his superior position. This shows how the workplace roles of speakers can influence the outcome of interactions like negotiations.

Nevertheless, we should not assume that the institutional roles of speakers always have a direct effect on how speakers interact. Roles and relationships can be negotiated through talk, and speakers may play different roles at different times. For example, in the encounter between Don and Andy it is noticeable that although Don is the subordinate, he does not assume a typically subordinate role. In fact, he argues more forcefully than Andy and also challenges him. It is perhaps interesting to know that Don is older than Andy and has worked in the office much longer. Factors like this may play an equally important role as the hierarchical status of speakers. We might even want to interpret Don's final comment (*you're the boss*) as a kind of indirect challenge to Andy's authority.

PROBLEM-SOLVING

Negotiating can be considered a sub-genre of a more general type of discourse: problem-solving. In fact, a great deal of workplace talk involves problem-solving of some kind. Problem-solving conversations often follow a problem-solution pattern. This is a textual pattern, which Hoey (2001) first identified in expository prose, and which has the following phases:

situation → problem → response/solution → evaluation

This means a problem is identified within a particular situation, then a response or solution is proposed, and finally this solution is evaluated positively or negatively. If the evaluation is negative, further solutions are proposed. According to Hoey, these phases are often signalled through the use of certain key words, such as:

◎   problem: *problem, difficult*;

◎   response/solution: *response, result, figure out*;

◎   evaluation: *work, good*.

Look at the following example from a problem-solving conversation, in which the speaker proposes how to solve a problem she has been discussing with a colleague:

so what we'll do is, let's you and me tomorrow sit down together and *try to wrack our brains* and *figure out* what's going on with each one of them.

The words and expressions *try*, *wrack our brains* and *figure out* are all clear signal words for the response/solution phase. Sometimes the signal words are not as obvious; for example **modal verbs** like *can*, *could*, or *need* can also play a role within a problem-solution pattern. In the example below, the modal verbs *will* and *be going to* are used by the same speaker as in the example above to say how she plans to solve the problem:

I mean *I'm gonna* go through and research, *I will* go through it with Becky, and *I'll* research as many as I can.

The use of these modals shows the speaker is quite confident that this is a good way to solve the problem. If she had used modals like *could* or *might* instead, the solution proposed would have sounded more tentative.

Look at Text 15: Green Envelope, which show a conversation between two speakers who work in the sales department of a British paper **supplier**. Greg is a sales rep and Bob is a senior sales rep and Greg's immediate manager. Greg is trying to get hold of a green envelope for a customer. The conversation begins with Greg asking Bob for some information, but it soon becomes clear that Greg has a problem. Read the transcript and answer the following questions:

◎   When do you think the presence of a problem is first signalled?

◎   What words and expressions does Bob use after this which point to a problem?

◎   When do you think the conversation moves to the response/solution phase and what words are used to signal this?

◎   Is a positive solution reached? What words are used that show positive or negative evaluation?

Text 15: Green Envelope

1	Greg	who's the one that does the Strange range.[4] Index[5] innit? ↓ that do those?
2	Bob	yeah what you after?
3	Greg	that's what I'm after trying to get the Pantone colour
4	Bob	right (.) so you need (.)
5	Greg	but no d– forget the Pantone bit now because the company–
6	Bob	⌊end of this week!
7	Greg	yeah the company I got it from last time *do* do it, but– they got to make it and it won't be till November
8	Bob	s– yeah.
9	Greg	yeah so basically I've just got to get (.) a green envelope pocket preferably gummed,
10	Bob	C5 green envelope

4 Strange range and Avalon range refer to types of paper.
5 Index, Belford, Waterford, Art and Design, C.S. Roth, Sanders and White are paper suppliers the company deals with (these are not the suppliers' real names).

11	Greg	⌊one–
12	Greg	one five one by two one six it is (.) I know that 'cause it's written in there
13	Bob	for C5.
14	Greg	for C5 yeah. so I'm just gonna go through 'em all
15	Bob	well there's not many people that'll make you a green envelope number one
16	Greg	⌊well there's Belford (.) but he's got one but it's a diamond flap an' he'd send it /??/ but I don't think it'd be good
17	Bob	I mean if you want something at the end of this week he's gonna struggle. uhm (.)
18	Greg	⌊yeah
19	Bob	↑you *might* find (.) ↓ Waterford's hang on
	(3)	[Bob reaches for a catalogue]
20	Greg	[yawns]
21	Bob	⌊that makes me strained. you– you– the only one you're gonna get's a C5 (1) ↑see we do a C5 in some of the Avalon range now ↓ don't do a *green* though, do we?
22	Greg	⌊No
23	Bob	how dark's the green?
24	Greg	⌊one five one by two one six is a standard size as well but it's (.) 'cause of the colour.
25	Bob	yeah the green's the one that's gonna be a killer
	(6)	[Greg hums]
26	Bob	Art an' Design do a C5 but do they do it in a green? no
27	Greg	we do it in a *dark* green but it's not what he wants I know it's a *bright* green that Pantone
28	Bob	how bright?
29	Greg	well (.)near enough fluorescent bright green
	(3)	[Bob typing on computer]
30	Bob	oh blimey. it's not–
31	Greg	⌊What– what Belford sent me it's like a (.) Christmassy green you know?
32	Bob	yeah I mean that's the sort of thing he– he'll find from stock unless you can persuade someone like (.) C.S. Roth to make it
33	Greg	⌊is–
34	Greg	could do, what sort of send him the paper?

35	Bob	⌊for next week
36	Greg	↑ that's a point yeah because–
37	Bob	⌊well no /??/
38	Greg	well no– yeah, Sanders an' White. i– I've got the paper he wants it's the colour /???/ ⌊Bob: ↓ Right⌋ an' they can send him the paper (.) C.S. Roth (2) be able to make it up
39	Bob	be an arm and a leg, but–
40	Greg	right haha /????????/ paper wouldn't they?
41	Bob	I'm surprised Sanders and White can't– we– with a– a– have you asked 'em if they could send it out to be made?
42	Greg	↑ oh well, they could send me the paper
43	Bob	they can *sell* you the paper yeah?
44	Greg	yeah they can sell me the paper on time /??/ he says to me I got (.) uh (.)
45	Bob	well speak to C.S. Roth. but C– I mean *I* had some envelopes made from C.S. Roth's the other day
46	Greg	oh yeah I suppose–
47	Bob	→ ⌊an' it took a couple of weeks but–

[Brief interruption while Bob speaks to another sales rep]

48	Bob	yeah I mean (.) C.S. Roth'll be able to make it
49	Greg	⌊↑ yeah 'cause i– uh i– uh I was gonna do that
50	Bob	'cause they can make the C5's (1) dead easy
51	Greg	⌊yeah I know he rung me back and he said to me to make– they've gotta get a job out by the end of the month. So they gotta do that within a week or it wouldn't go out till next week
52	Bob	yeah well C.S. Roth'll be able to make it
53	Greg	yeah /?/
54	Bob	certainly

(See the commentary at the end of this unit, pp. 72–3.)

This conversation shows how informal spoken genres develop out of the situation and are jointly 'negotiated'. The speakers don't set out to solve a problem at the beginning of the conversation; but one of the speakers, Bob, identifies a problem, which then leads to problem-solving.

Like the previous conversation we looked at (between Don and Andy), this one is also typical of a great deal of workplace talk, in that it is an 'unequal encounter' between a boss and a subordinate. Although problem-solving is basically a collaborative endeavour, Bob clearly plays a dominant role in this conversation: he identifies the presence of a problem and controls the direction the discourse takes. Greg certainly also plays an active role by responding to and commenting on Bob's suggestions, but it is Bob who proposes most of the solutions and evaluates the solution at the end. This can be explained in terms of his dominant position as Greg's boss, as well as his seniority and greater experience: he has been in the company longer, and thus knows the work much better than Greg does.

INSTRUCTIONS AND PROCEDURES

So far we have looked at workplace talk which is quite collaborative – where all speakers contribute more or less equally to the conversation. A great deal of workplace talk, however, involves telling other people what to do or explaining something; particularly in situations in which a new employee is being trained. In this type of talk, one speaker (the one giving the instructions or explaining the procedure) plays a dominant role in constructing the discourse. Conversations like this belong to the general category of **procedural** discourse, which is also an important written genre (see Unit six).

Activity

Look at the list of words and expressions below, and decide which ones you think a manager would use in giving instructions to a subordinate:

- ◎ Imperatives, e.g. '*Put* this over here.'
- ◎ you must
- ◎ you have to

◎   you should

◎   you can

◎   you want

◎   I would

◎   Let's

Text 16: Sorting Invoices shows extracts from a training session which took place in the back office of a North American organic food cooperative. The bookkeeper, Ann, is training her new assistant, Meg, and is explaining what to do with various documents, such as invoices.

Activity

Look at Text 16: Sorting Invoices and make a list of all the words and expressions Ann in fact uses for instruction-giving.

◎   Are they the same as in the list above?

◎   Is this what you expected or is there anything surprising?

◎   What general observation can you make about the way in which Ann gives instructions?

Text 16: Sorting Invoices

1	Ann	[going through files and papers as she speaks]
		okay so (.) in my files here (.) back here behind the (.) to be coded an' to be entered in the /????/ ↑ open credits ↓ an' packing slips[6] (.) so after you've got your pile of packing slips you open this up.
		what I've got is (.) invoices that have come in the mail that don't have any (.) don't have a– don't have a packing slip yet go in the left in alphabetical order ↑ and packing slips that have come from upstairs that don't have an invoice yet go on the right. so whenever

6 'Packing slip' or 'packing list': statement of the contents of a shipment usually put in or on the container or box.

		I get in a new one go to the: corresponding pile an' see if (.)
2	Meg	it's . . . in the other one
3	Ann	⌊ right. so (.) Save the Earth[7] (.) you know (.)
4	Meg	there it goes
5	Ann	there's that. the question is (.)
6	Meg	⌊ is whether they actually match?
7	Ann	yeah whether they (.) yeah. then the next thing you do is (.) ↑ there *should* also be a ↓ packing slip for this one here. so (.) I would do this (.) staple that bill of lading[8] onto that *in*voice 'cause we know *those* two go together
	(9)	
8	Meg	so they're all in this /?/
	(8)	
9	Ann	okay and (.) ↑ just– assuming that our packing slip's gonna come from upstairs ↓ you can go ahead an' put it back in here. an' then at– like at the end o' the month (.) we'll look through here an' say wait a second ↓ what happened to that packing slip an' figure it out then
10	Meg	⌊ okay (.) alright. an' then (.) other things I had /???/ this (.) uh– is this just a– d– do I just treat this–
11	Ann	hmmm (.) let's treat that as an invoice for one case at twenty-seven bucks an' that's it
12	Meg	⌊ okay
	[. . .]	
13	Ann	then (.) we wanna keep the two cover sheets (.) for that day's invoices (3) that's for ninety-three fifty an' ninety-three fifty-eight ↑ so basically you wanna see if you *have* those invoices already *in* here (.) an' then /????/ (.) fifty (.) got page seven, so you wanna make sure you got one through six here (.) ↓five, six ↑ page one doesn't really matter 'cause it's just the totes

(See the commentary at the end of this unit, pp. 73–5.)

---

7 'Save the Earth' is the name of a product range.
8 'Bill of lading': a document used in shipping goods.

The analysis of the training session with Ann and Meg shows that face-to-face procedural discourse involves a great deal more than a series of instructions (as you might find in written procedural discourse). The reason for this is that the speakers cannot ignore the interactive and interpersonal nature of a face-to-face encounter. Even in a situation like this, where one speaker plays a dominant role and does most of the talking, the dialogic nature of talk is evident. The dominant speaker seems to make an effort to make the discourse more interactive and less one-sided.

SUMMARY

The types of workplace interactions we have looked in this unit and their characteristics are summarized below:

◎ *Meetings* are highly structured and organized (often multi-party) interactions with a chair who opens and closes the meeting and guides the discussion. In order to do this job, the chair often uses metalanguage and discourse-organizing phrases.

◎ *Negotiations* involve two parties trying to reach a mutually satisfactory agreement about an issue where they have some differences. Negotiations usually go through a number of phases (information exchange, bidding, bargaining, settling and concluding) which are often signalled by discourse markers, intonation and pauses.

◎ *Problem-solving* is a collaborative activity which frequently follows a problem-solution pattern: situation → problem → response/solution → evaluation. The phases of this pattern are often signalled through the use of particular key words.

◎ In *procedural discourse* a dominant speaker gives instructions and explanations (often during training). Instruction-givers tend to use indirect language and avoid imperatives and modals of obligation.

Many workplace encounters involve unequal relationships, where one speaker is the hierarchical superior of another. As we have seen, this can influence the interaction in a number of ways, but it is not the only factor to affect the speakers' roles.

Extension

1   It is often difficult to get access to companies or organizations to make recordings of workplace interactions. However, if you have a part-time job, you may be able to record some conversations at work. If not, another source of authentic workplace conversations is TV documentaries or 'reality' programmes about office life. Record some spontaneous workplace interactions or a TV documentary which includes some unscripted talk in a workplace (i.e. not an interview conducted by the person making the documentary). Transcribe about ten minutes of the recording and analyse it, using the following questions as guidelines:

◎   Does the extract involve one of the types or genres of workplace discourse analysed in this unit?

◎   If so, does it display some of the characteristics of the genre identified in this unit?

◎   If you think it is a different type of workplace discourse, how is the discourse structured and what are some of the linguistic features?

2   If you are able to work in a group, organize a meeting to discuss a particular issue. You should work in a group of four to six people, with one person taking the role of chair and another the role of observer. The observer should make notes on the structure and language of the meeting, focusing on the following areas:

(a)   How does the chair organize the meeting and guide the discussion?

(b)   What metalanguage and discourse-organizing phrases does (s)he use?

(c)   What role do the other participants play?
◎   How do they take the floor?
◎   What kind of language do they use to give their opinions and argue their points.

When the meetings are finished, the observers from each group should report back to the class about their findings.

COMMENTARIES ON THE ACTIVITIES

Commentary on Text 13: Management Meeting (pp. 54–5)

The following metalinguistic phrases are used by Mike:

◎   topics I wanted to <u>handle</u>

◎   we gotta <u>talk about</u> that

◎   Bill would like to <u>propose</u>

◎   some other <u>ideas on the table</u>

◎   we should <u>deal with</u>

◎   hopefully we'll <u>get to</u> the other ones

Some of these are obviously metalinguistic, like *talk about* and *propose*, but others are perhaps less obvious. The verbs *handle* and *deal with* do not always refer to verbal activity, but in this context they do: the participants in the meeting will of course *handle* and *deal with* these things by talking about them. The expression *ideas on the table* is a metaphor for 'proposals' or 'suggestions', and is therefore also metalinguistic. The least obvious one is *get to*, which is of course primarily a verb of motion. But here it is used with the metaphorical meaning of 'have a chance to talk about'.

   Mike also uses the following discourse-organizing words and phrases to link the main ideas in his overview:

◎   that relates to the fact that

◎   that's– one thing

◎   the second thing is

◎   part of that has to do with

◎   and the other thing is

◎   the first thing

◎   here's the deal

Another discourse-organizing phrase he uses is *uhm so anyway* (Turn 8) in order to get back to his overview of the meeting after the interruption from Turns 2–7.

Commentary on Text 14: Negotiating about Applications
(pp. 58–9)

The negotiation between Don and Andy can be divided into the following phases:

1   exchanging information: Turns 1–5;

2   bidding: Turns 6;

3   bargaining: Turns 7–20;

4   settling and concluding: Turns 21–27;

5   re-opening bargaining: Turns 28–29;

6   settling and concluding: Turns 30–32.

This analysis of the structure of the negotiation shows that the phases do not always follow each other in a linear fashion. In this conversation Don re-opens bargaining in Turn 28, although in Turn 25 he has already agreed to do things Andy's way.

Commentary on Text 15: Green Envelope (pp. 63–5)

In Turn 15, Bob, the senior rep, first identifies a problem when he says:

> 15   Bob   well there's not many people that'll make you a green envelope number one

After this, Bob uses the following (underlined) words and expressions that explicitly signal a problem:

> 17   I mean if you want something at the end of this week he's gonna <u>struggle</u>

> 21   (. . .) <u>the only one</u> you're gonna get's a C5

> 25   yeah the green's the one that's gonna be <u>a killer</u>

> 39   be <u>an arm and a leg</u> but–

The conversation moves to the response phase from about Turn 32, although problems are still referred to later, for example in Turn 39 (shown above). Here Bob and Greg start to generate some ideas for a possible solution, and use words and expressions signalling a response (underlined):

> 32   Bob   (. . .) unless you <u>can persuade</u> someone like (.) C.S. Roth to make it

33	Greg	⌐Lis–
34	Greg	<u>could do</u>, what sort of send him the paper?
35	Bob	⌐for next week
36	Greg	↑ <u>that's a point</u> yeah because–
		(. . .)
41	Bob	I'm surprised Sanders and White can't– we– with a– a–
		<u>have you asked</u> 'em if they <u>could</u> send it out to be made?
42	Greg	↑ oh well they <u>could</u> send me the paper

Notice that they frequently use the modal verbs *can* and *could* to refer to possible solutions. Towards the end of the conversation, they use the modal verbs *will* and *be going to*:

48	Bob	yeah I mean (.) C.S. Roth<u>'ll be able</u> to make it
49	Greg	⌐↑yeah 'cause i– uh i– uh I was <u>gonna</u>
		do that

As these modals refer to the future, they are more assertive and less tentative than *can* and *could*. This shows how the response/solution phase of the conversation progresses from more tentative suggestions to firm decisions.

Finally, Bob evaluates the proposed solution positively by saying *dead easy* in Turn 50:

| 50 | Bob | 'cause they can make the C5's. (1) <u>dead easy</u> |

Commentary on Text 16: Sorting Invoices (pp. 67–8)

Here are the words and expressions used by Ann to give instructions:

Turn 1: <u>you open</u> this up
<u>packing slips</u> . . . <u>go</u> in the left . . . <u>go</u> on the right
<u>go</u> to the corresponding pile and <u>see</u> . . .

Turn 7: the next thing <u>you do</u> . . .
<u>I would do</u> this (.) <u>staple</u> that bill of lading . . .

Turn 9: <u>you can go ahead</u> and <u>put</u> . . .
<u>we'll look</u> through here . . . and <u>figure it out</u> then

Turn 11: <u>let's treat</u> that as . . .

Turn 13: <u>we wanna keep</u> . . .
<u>you wanna see</u> if . . .
<u>you wanna make</u> sure . . .

Here is the list of words and expressions you looked at before reading the transcript. The ones that are crossed out were *not* used:

Imperatives, e.g. '*Put* this over here.'

~~you must~~

~~you have to~~

~~you should~~

you can

you want

I would

let's

Ann does use *should* once, but this is to give background information, not to give a direct instruction:

Turn 7: there should also be a packing slip for this one here

Imperatives do occur (*go to the corresponding pile and see*), but not as much as one might expect in instruction-giving. Usually the verb used to give the instruction (*open, put, keep* etc.) is used together with something else. Sometimes *you* is used in front of the verb (*you open, you do*). This is known as the '*you*-imperative'. Sometimes a modal verb is used (e.g. *you can go ahead and put*). What may be surprising is that Ann uses *you wanna* (i.e. *you want to*) twice. This is not a verb we would normally associate with instruction-giving. It is even more surprising that she also says *we wanna*. In fact, on a number of occasions, Ann words her instructions as something she and Meg do together:

Turn 9: we'll look through here

Turn 11: let's treat that as . . .

And finally, on one occasion, Ann phrases her instructions as something she herself would do in the same situation:

Turn 7: I would do this (.) staple that bill of lading into that invoice

A general observation to be made about the way Ann gives instructions is that she does not use any expressions that refer to obligation or duty

(e.g. *you must, you have to, you should*), and she uses very few 'bare' imperatives (imperative verbs on their own). Instead she uses less direct formu-
lations in giving instructions, using other modal verbs (*you can, you wanna*)
and sometimes referring to joint action (*we wanna, let's*) or even to what
she herself would do. The overall effect it that Ann's instructions don't sound
like orders, and that she comes across as friendly and chatty. By using *we*
and *I*, as well as *you*, she makes the training session more interactive, and
avoids making it sound too much like a one-way transfer of information.

Relationships at work

The important role which the relationship between speakers and writers plays in the language of work has already been referred to in previous units. This unit will focus on relationships at work, exploring some of the ways in which the workplace or business relationship shapes the language used.

TASK GOALS AND RELATIONAL GOALS

In Unit one, we saw that one of the characteristics of workplace talk which distinguishes it from ordinary conversation is that speakers focus on specific tasks. However, not all communication that takes place at work is always about work; and even when it is, this does not mean that people always focus exclusively on the task at hand. Particularly in face-to-face conversations, people working together also need to take into account their relationship with each other while they are talking about work-related things. We can, therefore, say that people pay attention to relational goals as well as task goals when they are interacting for work or business.

Activity

Look at Text 17: Workplace Conversations, which shows three extracts from workplace conversations between co-workers, and answer the following questions:

◎ Which conversation is most task-focused and which is least task-focused?

◎ Which aspects of the language in each extract reflect a focus on the speakers' relational goals?

Text 17: Workplace Conversations

Conversation 1

1	Dave	basically I've used their old price list
2	Val	right
3	Dave	and (.) I've made a few changes
4	Val	yeah

Conversation 2

1	Rob	um I'm– I'm going white water rafting next– next weekend
2	Jim	*really!*
3	Rob	⌊so hopefully if I don't die I'll be back (.) the Monday after that
4	Jim	⌊hahahahahah haha

Conversation 3: Looking at something on the computer

1	Cathy	so that's what you want? Like a snapshot thing
2	Martha	⌊yeah.
3	Cathy	okay
4	Martha	⌊right okay .hh so ↑ boy it's tiny up there
5	Cathy	I know hehehe you need a big magnifying glass [chuckles]

(from the Cambridge International Corpus, © Cambridge University Press)

Commentary

Conversation 1 is the most task-focused of the three; in fact the two speakers focus exclusively on the task, which involves designing some brochures for a customer.

Conversation 2 is the least task-focused, and is in fact a typical example of 'small talk' with speakers talking about the weekend. The only indication that this conversation takes place at work between colleagues and not privately between friends is the mention of Monday, when the speakers will be back in the office after the weekend. Talking about the weekend and free time spent away from work is one way that people working together build relationships and bond, as this shows they are interested in each other as people, not just as co-workers. In particular the comment *really!* and the laughter, which show interest and appreciation, reflect a focus on relational goals.

In Conversation 3, the speakers are again engaged in a workplace task, however it is different from the first example, in that the comments in Turns 4 and 5 (about the size of the item on the computer screen) are not actually necessary for the task. These turns have some elements in common with the small talk in extract 2: we also find expressions of interest or surprise (*boy it's tiny up there*) as well as laughter. Comments like this about the task may not be necessary to get the job done, but they play an important role in building a positive relationship between people who work together.

BOSSES AND EMPLOYEES

Non-minimal responses

In Unit four we looked at procedural discourse involving instructions and explanations and saw how the language used by the instruction-giver showed an attention to the interactive and relational aspects of the encounter. Such a relational orientation can sometimes also be observed in the way the person being given the instructions responds.

Although the person who receives the instructions or explanations plays a less active role, it is nevertheless an important one, as it is essential that he or she understands the instructions. The role of 'listeners' may be limited to questions and **back channelling**, acknowledgements that they have understood, as is the case in the training session shown in Text 16: Sorting Invoices in Unit four. Meg, who is being trained in this conversation often simply says *okay* in response to her boss's instructions, e.g.:

11	Ann	hmmm (.) let's treat that as an invoice for one case at twenty-seven bucks an' that's it
12	Meg	⌊ okay,

We could call such back channelling a **minimal response**, as it is the minimum a listener needs to do to show that the message is being received. Other words used as minimal responses include: *mm, mhm, yes, yeah, right*. However, listeners in procedural discourse sometimes produce more than a minimal response.

Activity

Text 18: Nominal Printout shows the first part of a conversation between a professor and the department secretary in a British university. The professor, Hugh, has just taken over as head of department, and the secretary, Liz, is explaining a particular form (the 'nominal printout') to him. Read the transcript and answer the following questions:

◎ How does Hugh respond to Liz's instructions? Make a note of the different types of things he says.

◎ In what way are some responses 'non-minimal'? In other words, what do they add over and above simply acknowledging understanding?

◎ Why do you think Hugh uses **non-minimal responses** like this? How do they affect the interaction as a whole?

Text 18: Nominal Printout

1	Liz	understanding your nominal printout
2	Hugh	oh *yes* just what I *want*
3	Liz	that's how it comes, and then (.) (3) that carries on where the table goes off
4	Hugh	⌊ oh wonderful
5	Liz	and these are all the different things (.) that it could (.)
6	Hugh	oh *I* see, yeah

7	Liz	could end up as
8	Hugh	well that's– that–
9	Liz	⌊ right (.) So let me give you that, and then (.)
10	Hugh	do you want this back?
11	Liz	no no you can have that one
12	Hugh	⌊right
13	Hugh	okay
14	Liz	and if I give you (.) (10) [looks for forms] mm (2) if I give you a– a form like that that's *May '96* ⌊ Hugh: mhm, ⌋ *April '96 April 2 April* (.) *May* (.) (3) if I give you those to have a look through
15	Hugh	great yeah
	(1)	
16	Hugh	yes that's just– that's just around– yes alright okay
17	Liz	⌊that's another for May
18	Liz	these– these are all just our maintenance accounts
19	Hugh	yeah fine yeah that– that'll be
20	Liz	oh that's the– oh– this is before they started to back things up
21	Hugh	⌊↓ just what I want
22	Liz	we now have things–⌊Hugh: mm⌋ backed up[1] instead of single sheets (.) that's right then we go onto the June ones yeah
23	Hugh	backed up?
24	Liz	I– like this now (.) oh (.) ↑hm
	(1.5)	
25	Hugh	oh I *see* ↓yeah yeah.
26	Liz	they used to send them on single sheets but now they
27	Hugh	⌊yeah yeah yeah.
28	Liz	back everything up for us
29	Hugh	oh great

(See the commentary at the end of this unit, p. 94–5.)

---

1 By 'backed up' Liz means double-sided, as she goes on to show Hugh in Turn 24.

Text 18: Nominal Printout shows that when people work together on a regular basis, they do seem to make an effort to build a positive working relationship, and this is reflected in the language they use. But the precise nature of that relationship in terms of the speakers' workplace roles and relative power is also important and has an effect on the discourse. As we have already seen in previous units, many workplace interactions involve 'unequal encounters' between a hierarchically more powerful manager and a subordinate. In Text 16: Sorting Invoices, in Unit four, a bookkeeper gives instructions to her assistant, and in Text 18: Nominal Printout, it is the person with a more subordinate position (the secretary) who gives instructions to someone higher up in the hierarchy (the professor).

It is interesting that Hugh, the professor, uses non-minimal responses, whereas Meg, the assistant does not, as the extract below from another part of their conversation (not shown in Unit four) illustrates:

1	Ann	↑ uhm (.) *that* is for the Save the Earth stuff, and (.) I will– it will *even*tually probably get thrown away, but (.) if you haven't come across a packing ↑list for Save the Earth products
2	Meg	<u>okay</u>
3	Ann	hang onto it
4	Meg	<u>okay</u>

This can be explained in terms of the respective roles and work relationships in each of the two encounters. Hierarchical relationships imply certain duties and obligations, and one of the duties of bosses is that they should tell their subordinates what to do, especially if they are new (as in the case of Meg). Training and giving instructions is therefore what is expected of a superior, and this could explain why Meg almost exclusively produces minimal responses (or asks questions). Ann, who is training her, is only doing her job, and therefore probably does not expect Meg to show any special appreciation, for example through non-minimal responses.

The situation with Hugh and Liz is different. He is the head of the department, and is therefore expected to know what is involved in running the department (but being new, there is of course a lot he does not know). One could see Liz's helping him with his new job as a kind of favour; and therefore it seems appropriate that he should express appreciation for her help. In addition, his non-minimal responses could have the function of encouraging Liz in her current role as instruction-giver, which, as Hugh's subordinate, she is probably not used to.

DEALING WITH PROBLEMS

So far we have looked at how people working together contribute to a positive relationship through small talk, non-minimal responses, humour and by generally showing interest in and appreciation of what the other person says. However, things do not always go smoothly at work, and being positive is not necessarily an appropriate reaction when things go wrong. The following activity looks at a manager dealing with a situation in which an employee has made a mistake.

Activity

Text 19: Lost Order took place in the sales office of a British company that sells paper. One of the sales reps, Mark, tells his boss, Paul, that he has lost a substantial order because a competitor offered the customer a better price. Look at what Paul, the office manager says, and answer the following questions:

◎   How does Paul react to Mark's news that he has lost the order?

◎   What kinds of words and expressions does he use from Turn 10 onwards in commenting on what has happened?

◎   Why do you think he uses these expressions in the current situation?

Text 19: Lost Order

1	Mark	we lost that one (.) that /??/ one
2	Paul	↑did we?
3	Mark	yeah someone quoted seven hundred pound a ton
4	Paul	on what
5	Mark	⌊didn't say well (.) say equivalent sheet but (.) as far as *I* was aware we was the only ones who could get hold of Sienna Print[2]
6	Paul	no various mills (.) various merchants can get hold of it
7	Mark	just (.) they call it something else yeah
8	Paul	yeah Terra Print or whatever
9	Mark	yeah
10	Paul	that's a bit of a *pain* isn't it
11	Mark	yeah so (.) so–

2 'Sienna Print' and 'Terra Print' are types of paper.

83

12	Paul	⌊remember that next time
13	Mark	I said to him uh (.) let us know next time you know (.) what (.) prices you're getting in and we'll always see if we can better (.) that /?/
14	Paul	well you'll know it for next time
15	Mark	mm
16	Paul	[funny voice] trying to be too greedy
	(2)	
17	Mark	mm
18	Paul	⌊well I m– we won't– y' know don't know do yous
19	Mark	you don't know
	(3)	
20	Mark	well it's annoying that he's got an order in if you think about it at forty pound a ton or whatever
	[. . .]	
21	Paul	mm
22	Mark	it's not exactly like not getting an order at all though
23	Paul	⌊annoying innit
	(3)	
24	Mark	that would have been quite nice
25	Paul	oh well
	(11)	
26	Paul	it's a pain, isn't it
27	Mark	mm
	(1.5)	
28	Paul	can't win 'em all
	(9)	
29	Paul	about a *grand* that isn't it
	[. . .]	
30	Mark	yeah
31	Paul	oh well
	(4)	
32	Paul	win some you lose some so (1.5) we coulda made seven hundred quid out of it couldn't we
	(1)	
33	Mark	mm
34	Paul	oh well
	(2.5)	
35	Paul	it's an*noy*in' though innit hhh

(See the commentary at the end of this unit, pp. 95–6.)

POLITENESS AND 'FACE'

The notions of 'saving face' and 'keeping face' are central in examining language and relationships between people. Brown and Levinson (1987) have developed a theory of how the notion of **face**, which has to do with basic human needs and feelings of self-worth, influences how people interact. According to Brown and Levinson (p. 62) every member of society has two opposing types of needs or wants:

negative face: the want of every 'competent adult member' that his actions be unimpeded by others.

positive face: the want of every member that his wants be desirable to at least some others.

Positive or negative face can be threatened in various interactive situations by what Brown and Levinson call **face-threatening acts**. Negative face is threatened by impositions from others, involving, for example, requests or orders, and positive face is threatened by acts like criticism or disagreement. When face-threatening acts cannot be avoided, speakers try to mitigate their impact by using a variety of verbal strategies frequently involving indirectness. Brown and Levinson call such interactive strategies 'positive' and 'negative **politeness**', depending on whether positive or negative face is being saved.

In the conversation between Paul and Mark about the lost order (Text 19), recriminations or criticisms from the boss (Paul) represent a threat to the subordinate's (Mark) positive face. By avoiding direct criticism and using more indirect ways of evaluating what has happened, Paul uses positive politeness strategies.

RELATIONSHIPS WITH CUSTOMERS

Up till now in this unit we have looked at relationships between co-workers, in particular 'asymmetrical' relationships between managers and subordinates, where one person is in a position of power in relation to the other within a particular organization. Another important type of workplace relationship is that between service providers or suppliers and customers. This is again an asymmetrical kind of relationship, but not because of any kind of direct institutional power of one person over the other. But generally speaking customers are in a more powerful position, as they can choose to buy or not to buy the product or service being offered.

Activity

The extract shown in Text 20: Meeting with Supplier is from the beginning of a meeting between Paul, the office manager from the last conversation, and a supplier, Angus. Paul works in a small branch of a company that sells paper to printers. Angus, who works for one of their suppliers, a wholesale distributor of paper, visits Paul's branch. They have done business together in the past and have met before, but most of their contact is on the telephone. Angus has come to tell Paul about some of his company's current offers and services with a view to trying to get some more business from Paul's company. Look at the Text and answer the following questions:

◎   What linguistic strategies do the speakers use that make their language more indirect?

◎   Which of the speakers uses them most?

◎   Are they mainly positive or negative politeness strategies?

◎   Why do you think they use these strategies?

Text 20: Meeting with Supplier

1	Angus	uh ↓ just wanted to come and chat to you a little bit about the company 'cause the– paper brokers have changed a little bit
2	Paul	oh yeah? what you been up to then?
3	Angus	uhm (.) well I– I did quite a bit with Tony Reilly and ⌊Paul: mm⌋ Stan White um centrally and uh (.) we used to do quite a bit– with you as well ↓ Uhm (.) but at least i–
4	Paul	⌊↑ yeah but a lot– ↓th– one of the sort of funny things with this /??????/
5	Angus	right
	(2)	
6	Paul	we t– there's a fair amount of sort of (.) standard stuff at Belvedere we can– take it from there but–
7	Angus	⌊that's right ⌊yes (1) yup
	[3]	
8	Angus	but uhm
	[Interruption while Paul finishes some work at his computer]	

9	Angus	right. ↑ we uhm (.) we faxed another clearance list
10	Paul	⌊yeah we get that
11	Angus	you get that
12	Paul	yeah we get that
13	Angus	⌊uhm (.) it's really just an attempt to show you what kind of– what kind of stock we've got ⌊Paul: Mm⌋ and (.) I know that uhm you would– prefer draw from Belvedere
14	Paul	↑ yeah ↓ I mean we're– we're not fussed really
15	Angus	no
16	Paul	depends where we get our best price from really [chuckles]
17	Angus	ah right well
18	Paul	heheheheh
19	Angus	I'm your man

(See the commentary at the end of this unit, pp. 96–8.)

According to Brown and Levinson, positive politeness can be used not only to mitigate a face-threatening act, for example to soften criticism (as in Text 19: Lost Order), but also to show a more general appreciation for the other's wants. One such positive politeness strategy is 'claiming common ground', that is saying something which indicates that you and the addressee have something in common or are part of the same group.

Activity

Look at Text 20: Meeting with Supplier again, and identify any positive politeness strategies which you think Paul and Angus use to claim common ground.

(See the commentary at the end of this unit, pp. 96–8.)

The use of positive and negative politeness strategies in the meeting between Paul and Angus clearly indicates that the relationship plays an important role in the way the two speakers interact. Their language is not simply oriented towards getting the business done, but shows their attention to relational goals. Their different use of politeness strategies reflects the different roles they play in the meeting: Angus, as the supplier, wants something from Paul (more business), and is thus in a less powerful position. Therefore he uses a great number of negative politeness strategies to try to mitigate the imposition of trying to get more business out of Paul. Paul uses negative politeness for a different purpose: to protect his freedom as buyer to get his business from where he wants. Both speakers use positive politeness by claiming common ground, and the purpose of this seems to be to build a positive working relationship. This indicates that this is a business relationship both the supplier and customer are interested in maintaining.

SERVICE ENCOUNTERS

Another type of encounter in which sales people or service providers interact with customers is in situations involving members of the general public. Such interactions are referred to as **service encounters**. The service industry has grown considerably over the last decade or so, and a large number of everyday services, such as banking or booking holidays, can now be handled over the telephone. This has given rise to call centres, which deal exclusively with telephone service encounters. They are now so widespread that we are all familiar with such telephone conversations with agents working in call centres.

Activity

Based on your own experience as a customer in telephone service encounters (for example: calling Directory Enquiries; querying a bill; booking a train ticket) make a note of all the things you can think of that the agents you have spoken to typically say.

Check your answers at the end of this unit (p. 99), before you read the commentary below.

Commentary

You were probably able to come up with at least three or four things that agents in telephone service encounters typically say, regardless of the type of service involved. This is because much of the language in such telephone conversations is highly formulaic, rather than spontaneous. When we are engaged in these conversations, we are aware of the fact that they are not like 'normal' conversations, but that very often the agent is following some kind of script, and is supposed to say certain things, for example in beginning and ending the call.

Deborah Cameron (2000: 96), who studied call centre interactions, notes that the questions asked by agents, and the order in which they are asked, are determined by the software they are working with. They need to elicit information from the caller and input it into the computer in a specific order. Eliciting information efficiently is, however, not the only consideration. The customer should also feel he or she has been given good service, and therefore some of the things the agent says have to do with the interpersonal or relational aspects of the encounter.

Activity

Look at the extract shown in Text 21: Investment Firm Telephone Conversation, taken from a telephone service encounter involving a North American investment firm. To protect the anonymity of the speakers, specific details of the transaction cannot be given, but for our purposes it is enough to know that the customer has invested some money with the firm, and in this conversation wants to set up a new account. Note that the beginning of the call is missing. Look at the Text and answer the following questions:

◎ Which questions or other contributions of the agent do you think are necessary for the transaction, i.e. for her to input information into her system or process the transaction?

◎ Which of the agent's contributions have more to do with relationship-building with the caller as a customer?

◎ To what extent would you say that these contributions actually contribute to building a relationship with the customer and providing a good service?

Text 21: Investment Firm Telephone Conversation

Jenny: agent of investment firm
Mary: caller and customer of investment firm

1	Jenny	and could you give me the account number?
2	Mary	yes it's 629 ⌊Jenny: mhm⌋ 378 ⌊Jenny: mhm⌋ 30 59
3	Jenny	okay, just a minute (.) 629, 378, 30 59 yeah? okay and your name?
4	Mary	Mary Simmons
5	Jenny	okay (.) uhm do you have another account with us?
6	Mary	no
7	Jenny	okay this is the only one you have with us?
8	Mary	yup
9	Jenny	okay (.) what did you– did you want to create a new account with us?
10	Mary	yeah a new account with [. . .]
11	Jenny	okay, and have you read the prospectus.
12	Mary	yeah
13	Jenny	okay (.) now you need to stay on the line with me while we process this
14	Mary	okay
15	Jenny	all right (1) okay could you give me your current address please?
16	Mary	yeah sure it's uh 29 Rosewood Lane ⌊Jenny: mhm⌋ in Valparaiso Indiana.
17	Jenny	okay. and the zip code there?
18	Mary	46375
19	Jenny [. . .]	okay, and could you give me [. . .]?
20	Jenny	okay mhm and a phone number where you can be reached during the day
21	Mary	yeah 219 ⌊Jenny: mhm⌋ 467 ⌊Jenny: mhm⌋ 3252 ⌊Jenny okay⌋ (.) just a minute more [. . .] I'll put this through for you now
22	Mary [. . .]	okay
23	Jenny	[. . .] but you can call up tomorrow for confirmation, but you will also be receiving written confirmation in the mail

24	Mary	okay great
25	Jenny	okay? and something else I can help you with?
26	Mary	No that's it
27	Jenny	okay well thanks for calling Ms Simmons
28	Mary	bye bye
29	Jenny	bye bye now

Check your answers at the end of this unit (pp. 99–100), before you read the commentary below.

Commentary

Both the task-oriented parts of the agent's discourse as well as the ones with a relational focus could form part of her script for conversations with customers. We do not know exactly what guidelines she is following, but many features of this conversation, for example the elaborate closing, are typical for telephone service encounters, and thus are likely to form part of the 'routine' of such conversations. This raises the question of what kind of 'relationship' actually exists between the server and the customer in such interactions. Usually, these telephone conversations are 'one-off' encounters, as the customer is unlikely to speak to the same agent twice. In addition, agents working in call centres will repeat similar conversations with a large number of different callers in the course of a day. From the company's point of view, the telephone agents act as representatives of the firm, and therefore if the customer is satisfied with the service received during such telephone encounters, this should foster a long-term relationship with the customer. However, if relationally-oriented language is simply part of a script (and this is something customers will notice), the question then is whether politeness formulae such as *how may I help you* actually still perform any kind of interpersonal function, or whether they are not then just empty phrases.

Cameron (2000) goes even further in taking a critical view of the language of call centre telephone interactions. She concludes that such interactions are subject to a worrying degree of managerial control, characterized by 'codification' and 'surveillance' (2000: 98). Her research shows that many call centres give very detailed specifications, or even full scripts, for what the telephone agent should say, and that telephone calls are monitored and recorded, and used as a basis for appraisal. This, she says, results in a standardization of interactions and a reduction of the autonomy of

91

the call centre employees. She concludes that call centres are 'communication factories', with employees working in conditions similar to a production line.

Cameron leaves us with a fairly grim view of the language of work in call centres. It is, of course, important to take a critical view of workplace communication in all kinds of contexts, and to examine the types of power relationships that the language may reveal. But not all telephone service interactions are necessarily as routine and repetitive as Cameron suggests. Telephone agents do also sometimes have to handle more unusual situations, and occasionally there is even opportunity for genuine interpersonal communication between server and customer. Cheepen (2000), who looked at small talk in telephone service dialogues, gives the following example of a conversation, where the server actually interrupts the transaction with a genuine enquiry about the caller's health (underlined portions of the text).

Text 22: Electricity Provider Telephone Conversation

A = agent
C = customer

1	A	but you said something about you wanted to change the change the
2		name Miss Ward
3	C	yeh the name should now be it's Mrs M Franton. now
4	A	Mrs
5	C	M Franton
6	A	Franton
7	C	F R A N T O N
8	A	T O N
9	C	yes – <u>you sound full of cold</u>
10	A	<u>do I</u>
11	C	<u>yes</u>
12	A	<u>yes yes I've started with a bit of one yeh</u>
13	C	<u>(laugh)</u>
14	A	<u>keep smiling for me and I might not get one</u>
15	C	<u>(laugh)</u>
16	A	<u>(laugh)</u> I'll do that for you then Mrs M Franton and I'll send you a
17		direct debit mandate out for twenty-one pounds

(Cheepen 2000: 303–4)

SUMMARY

This unit has explored a number of different types of workplace relationships:

◎ people working together in the same organization, in particular supervisors and subordinates;

◎ suppliers and customers working within the same branch of industry;

◎ service providers and customers who are members of the general public, in particular in telephone service encounters.

The nature of each of these relationships is reflected in and shapes the language used in interactions.

We have also seen that certain things people say in workplace encounters have more to do with the relational rather than the task goals of the speakers. These include:

◎ Non-minimal responses, which listeners use not only to demonstrate understanding, but also to show appreciation and express other more affective meanings.

◎ Positive and negative politeness, which speakers use to protect their own and the other's 'face'. Politeness strategies include using idioms (in particular proverbs or maxims), hedges and other indirectness devices, and claiming common ground, for example through the use of colloquial vocabulary.

◎ Expressions and phrases used by telephone agents which are designed to show politeness towards the customer and thus provide good service.

Examining the language of work in terms of relationships also allows us to take a critical look at the inequalities and issues of power that characterize many workplace relationships.

Extension

1   Many television programmes deal with either fictional or real workplace situations, some taking a humorous or satirical view, such as the popular series 'The Office'. Record a documentary or an episode from a serial, and transcribe a short extract which involves interaction either between a boss and an employee or a sales person/server and customer. Analyse the transcript in terms of the relationship between the speakers. What does the language they use tell you about their relationship? For example, who uses more positive or negative politeness strategies? If it is a fictional, scripted dialogue, how have the writers portrayed this particular kind of workplace relationship. Positively? Negatively?

2   You probably engage in service encounters of one type or another on a daily basis. It may not be possible to go around with a portable tape recorder, recording all your interactions, but you can make a note of some of what was said while it is still fresh in your mind. After you have been to a shop, your bank, or spoken to someone in a call centre, make a note of some of the things that the server has said. Which of the things he/she said were necessary to complete the transaction? Which do you think fulfilled more of a relational function?

COMMENTARIES ON AND ANSWERS TO THE ACTIVITIES

Commentary on Text 18: Nominal Printout (pp. 80–1)

Hugh responds in a number of different ways. He uses some minimal responses:

◎   right

◎   yeah

◎   okay

He also asks some questions:

◎   Turn 10: do you want this back?

◎   Turn 23: backed up?

He frequently uses non-minimal responses:

◎   oh wonderful

◎   oh I see

◎   fine

◎   just what I want

◎   (oh) great

Sometimes these non-minimal responses are incomplete, e.g.:

◎   Turn 8: well that's that–

Except for *I see*, the non-minimal responses do more than simply acknowledge understanding: they express satisfaction, enthusiasm, as well as humour. *Oh wonderful* and *just what I want* are certainly meant somewhat ironically, as having a form explained is obviously not the most exciting thing in the world. By showing his appreciation for Liz's explanations, and by injecting a bit of humour into this fairly dry activity, Hugh makes the whole interaction more friendly and congenial. So non-minimal responses are not necessary for simply getting the job done; but, as McCarthy and Carter (2000) say, they 'serve important interactive and affective functions' because they contribute to a good relationship between the speakers.

Commentary on Text 19: Lost Order (pp. 83–4)

Paul first explains that, contrary to what Mark thought, their company is not the only supplier for the type of paper the customer wanted (which is why the customer was able to get it cheaper elsewhere), but that the paper is sold under a different name (Turns 5–8). He then remarks that Mark will know this for next time (Turns 12 and 14), and therefore presumably will not make the same mistake again, but will try to offer the customer a better price. From Turn 10 onwards both speakers make comments which express their frustration that they did not get the order, for example:

22   Mark   it's not exactly like not getting an order at all /though/
23   Paul   ⌊annoying innit

In doing this, Paul uses a number of different types of words and expressions. He repeats *it's annoying* and *it's a pain* to express how they presumably both feel about losing the order:

◎   Turn 23: annoying innit

◎   Turn 35: It's an*noy*in' though innit hhh.

◎   Turn 10: that's a bit of a *pain* isn't it

◎   Turn 26: it's a pain isn't it

Notice that Paul avoids directly attributing blame to Mark, by using the neutral pronoun '*it*', e.g. *it's annoyin'* (Turn 35).

What is particularly striking is his frequent use of a particular type of **idiom** – proverbial expressions or 'maxims', which seem to express the general wisdom that these kinds of things just happen sometimes:

◎   Turn 18: don't know do yous

◎   Turn 28: can't win 'em all

◎   Turn 32: win some you lose some

The function of all the above expressions is to evaluate this negative turn of events. The question is why Paul should so frequently use idioms like this. Maxims like *can't win 'em all* are obviously not original, and are there-fore often referred to as 'clichés'. We use expressions like this to refer to some vague but generally recognized 'wisdom' in our culture. As Rosamund Moon (1992) says, proverbs and maxims allow speakers to 'shelter behind shared values' (p. 24). And it is precisely because they are not original that Paul uses such expressions here: they allow him to evaluate the situation without directly blaming Mark.

This encounter involves a particularly delicate situation, where a subordinate (Mark) has admitted to a mistake. By referring to how they both feel (*it's annoying*, *it's a pain*) and using placating, generalizing maxims (e.g. *win some you lose some*) Paul allows Mark to save face. Note that the only direct reference to what Mark may have done wrong is spoken with a 'funny' voice, which indicates that he is not being serious: *trying to be too greedy* (Turn 16).

Commentary on Text 20: Meeting with Supplier (pp. 86–7)

The speakers use the following linguistic strategies to make their language more indirect:

1   Adverbial **hedges**: these are adverbs, such as *quite* or *really*, which have little meaning on their own, but which make the message more 'fuzzy' or indirect.

The following adverbial hedges are used:

◎ just (Turns 1 and 13)

◎ a little bit (Turn 1)

◎ quite a bit (Turn 3)

◎ sort of (Turn 4 and 6)

◎ really (13, 14 and 16)

2 The past tense: 'just <u>wanted to</u>' (Turn 1): here the past tense (*wanted*) is not used to refer to past time, but simply for politeness. This involves a kind of metaphorical use of the past tense: just as a past event is temporally removed from the present, so it can function as an interpersonal distancing device between the speaker and the hearer.

Angus, the supplier, uses these indirectness devices much more than Paul, the customer. Notice how he frequently uses a number of them together, e.g.:

◎ Turn 1: <u>just wanted to</u> come and chat to you <u>a little bit</u> about the company.

◎ Turn 13: it's <u>really just</u> an attempt to show you what kind of– what kind of stock we've got.

The reason Angus uses these devices is to minimize the imposition which his visit to the customer represents. In his role as supplier, he is the one who wants something from the customer. This involves a kind of threat to the customer's negative face, therefore these devices are all negative politeness strategies.

Another negative politeness strategy used by Angus is to be pessimistic and not assume that the customer wants to buy from him, for example when he says, in Turn 13, *I know that uhm you would– prefer draw from Belvedere*.

Although Angus uses most of the hedges, Paul uses a few as well, e.g.:

◎ Turn 6: there's a fair amount of <u>sort of</u> (.) standard stuff at Belvedere we can– take it from there

◎ Turn 14:

13 Angus ... I know that uhm you would– prefer draw from Belvedere

14 Paul I mean we're– we're not fussed <u>really</u>

In both these examples, the fact is alluded to that Paul's sales office can draw a number of supplies directly from the company warehouse (Belvedere). The use of hedges allows Paul to be more vague about where he gets his supplies and what he gets. This is also an example of negative politeness, but here it is used by Paul to protect his own 'face' and retain his freedom of action.

Positive politeness (p. 88)

One positive politeness strategy both speakers employ is the use of informal, colloquial vocabulary and expressions:

◎   chat (Turn 1)

◎   what you been up to (Turn 2)

◎   stuff (Turn 6)

◎   we're not fussed (Turn 14)

The use of colloquial language like this in a business situation involves claiming common ground, as this kind of language signals a certain degree of familiarity, even closeness, between the two speakers.

The use of humour and laughter in Turns 16–19 clearly has a similar function:

16   Paul   depends where we get our best price from really
              [chuckles]
17   Angus   ah right well
18   Paul   heheheheh
19   Angus   I'm your man

Note how Angus uses an idiom (*I'm your man*) to claim common ground in Turn 19.

It is interesting that many of the adverbial hedges (*just, sort of, really*) identified above as having a negative politeness function also contribute to the informality of the language used. That is, they simultaneously perform positive and negative politeness functions.

Answers to Activity: What telephone agents typically say
(p. 88)

Here are some of the things call centre agents typically say:

◎   Good morning/afternoon. This is X speaking. How can/may I help you?

◎   Could you give me your account/customer number, please?

◎   Can I have your name, please?

◎   One moment, please.

◎   I'll just put you on hold.

◎   Sorry to keep you waiting

◎   I'll put you through to X.

◎   Is there anything else I can do for you?

◎   Thank you for calling.

Answers for Text 21: Investment Firm Telephone Conversation
(pp. 90–1)

Jenny, the agent, has to elicit the following information from the customer, Mary:

◎   Her account number (Turn 1)

◎   Her name (Turn 3)

◎   Whether she already has another account with the firm (Turns 5 and 7)

◎   What the customer would like to do (Turn 9)

◎   The customer's address and daytime telephone number (Turns 15–18)

The question in Turn 11, asking whether the customer has read the prospectus, also seems to be important information for Jenny. However, we can't be sure whether she simply needs to tick a box in her system, or whether she would have been required to explain the conditions of the account had the customer said no.

The following parts of the agent's discourse relate to relational aspects of the encounter.

During various parts of the transaction Mary, the caller, has to wait while Jenny inputs information into her computer or waits for data to be processed. When this happens, she indicates this to Mary, saying *just a minute* (Turn 3) or *just a minute more* (Turn 21). This serves the purpose of explaining pauses in the conversation, and thereby showing politeness or respect towards the caller. Similarly in Turn 13 Jenny says: *now you need to stay on the line with me while we process this*. Here there is no pause in the conversation, but this serves as a kind of advance warning or excuse for keeping the caller on the phone for a while longer.

In a similar vein, Jenny also sometimes explains what she is going to do or what the customer should expect as a result of the telephone transaction:

◎   Turn 21: I'll put this through for you now

◎   Turn 23: but you can call up tomorrow for confirmation, but you will also be receiving written confirmation in the mail

None of this is actually necessary for Jenny to complete the transaction, but keeping the customer informed is part of the good service that she is expected to give.

And finally, the fairly elaborate closing also reflects the relational focus on politeness and providing good service. Before ending the call, the agent asks whether the customer would like any other service, and then thanks her for her call:

◎   Turn 25: and something else I can help you with?

◎   Turn 28: okay well thanks for calling Ms Simmons.

Entering the job market

This book has looked at a variety of texts from different workplace contexts, and the final unit now examines texts relevant to the topic of entering the world of work. As in previous units, the aim will be to analyse the language of the texts, and not to provide actual help or advice on getting a job. Nevertheless, it is hoped that these texts will provide a useful introduction to this topic for readers who are currently or will soon be entering the job market.

HELP WITH THE JOB HUNT

If you are trying to enter the job market for the first time, for example after school or university, there is no shortage of help and advice available from a variety of sources: careers advisers, job fairs, books and manuals on applying for a job, as well as articles in newspapers and magazines on the topic. The first activity in this unit, looks at a number of texts of this type.

Texts giving advice and guidelines on getting a job fall into the general category of 'procedural genres' – texts dealing with instructions or procedures of some kind. In Units four and five we looked at spoken procedural texts in workplace situations, in which particular work procedures and documents were explained to a co-worker. This unit examines the characteristics of a number of written procedural texts, and the extent to which they are similar to or different from spoken procedural texts.

Below you will find three texts which all give advice of some kind to people trying to get a job, in particular university graduates. Two texts are from the 'Rise' section of the *Guardian*, which is a special section of the newspaper for graduates, and one is from a magazine on work experience published by the National Council for Work Experience. The first text is an extract from an article which gives guidelines on different aspects of the job search, including CV writing, writing a cover letter and interviews. The second takes the form of an 'Agony Aunt' column, in which readers can write in and ask for advice on any aspect of looking for a job. The third one uses an 'FAQ' ('Frequently Asked Questions') format, a popular type of text found in many different contexts, in particular on websites.

Activity

Look at Texts 23 to 25: Help with the Job Hunt, and answer the following questions:

◎   What is the format of each text and why do you think this format was chosen? You should include:

  –   The physical layout.

  –   The role of the reader/addressee.

◎   How does each text give advice?

  –   Are imperatives used?

  –   Are modal verbs used? If so, which ones?

  –   Do you notice any other grammatical structures?

◎   How can you account for the differences between the texts?

102

Ready for lift off?

WELCOME to Guardian Graduate Month – four weeks of information, advice and opinion to help you launch your career. Ian Wylie begins the countdown.

Remember what you promised yourself at the start of the year? You'd focus on your finals, then kick-start your career search in June. Sounded a great plan five months ago, but now that the sun is shining, your friends are throwing frisbee in the park and the kebabs are sizzling on the BBQ . . . It's time to get your job-hunting fit for the summer with this 30-day plan:

The job search

1. Take responsibility. Accepting ownership for the progress of your job search is crucial.

2. Start a daily log of your job-searching activities and regularly assess your progress.

3. Take control: an aggressive job hunt will only work if you're in complete control. Choose a handful of target companies.

4. Research as much as you can about your target companies. Know their business inside out by reading the business pages and industry magazines.

5. Get to know the key people through news stories and features, corporate websites, press releases and personal contacts.

6. Contact your target manager or recruiter. Ask for an informational interview or, if you have the manager on the line, a short meeting. At the very least, get a commitment that they will read your CV and covering letter.

The CV

7. Choose between a functional CV and a chronological one. In functional CVs, you herd your skills into categories then briefly list past job titles at the bottom. If you're a typical graduate, stick with the chronological format, listing your jobs (and duties for each) in reverse chronological order.

8. Categorize your achievements, outlining sections of your experience, education and skills to explain what you've accomplished.

9. Make it look good. Along with effective organization, appearance can make or break your CV.

10. Keep your font plain and easy to read, whether you email, fax, or post your CV. Use a sans serif font like Arial or Verdana, not Times New Roman. These are much clearer when faxed.

. . .

Guardian, Saturday May 31, 2003

Text 24: Help with the Job Hunt – Ask Rise

Ask Rise

I'm a maths graduate and would love to work as a buyer in the retail clothing sector. Is it impossible for someone with my academic background to break into this type of work?
BS, Leeds

Everything is possible if you're determined enough. Some recruiters stipulate a degree such as fashion as a prerequisite, but they're open to hearing why you would be equally good.

Others like Debenhams consider students from all disciplines, but if there isn't an obvious link between your study and their business needs you'll have to make a strong case for why they should consider you.

Many companies do initial applications sifts using a points system; so much for your degree, and so much for other characteristics and experiences. If you're not going to score highly on subject, you must make it up elsewhere. Put yourself inside the recruiter's head; they'll want to know how past and present experiences prove your passion for fashion.

You must demonstrate a clear understanding of what the role of buyer involves. The most effective way of acquiring that is through work experience or shadowing. You should also seek out buyers, suppliers, people working in fashion houses and talk to them about their work. This needs to be complemented by research that equips you with informed opinions on what works and what doesn't, how catwalk clothes convert into high street sellers, who has the best window displays, what caused the last big flop, what might be the next big thing and why.

Got a career problem? Ask Rise by emailing irenek@lycos.co.uk

Guardian, Saturday May 31, 2003

Text 25: Help with the Job Hunt –
Work Experience FAQs

Work experience
FAQs

Philip Donnelly, Managing Director, STEP Enterprise Ltd

Do employers really want work experience. Isn't a degree enough?

So many people have degrees these days that you will need to stand out from the crowd when applying for jobs. Employers are increasingly demanding that new recruits are able to add value straight away. If you can demonstrate that you have already achieved a certain level of competence you will be far more likely to get the job you want.

Why should I be thinking about work experience this early?

It's never too early to start thinking about your options. You can use your time at university get a range of useful experiences that will stand you in good stead later. Remember that your top priority in your final year may be your final exams or coursework, so you don't have long to turn yourself into a marketable commodity.

. . .

Is one form of work experience more valuable than another?

If you can get structured, project-based work experience, so much the better, but you can learn a lot in any working environment.

You might work over the summer holidays, or during the weekends, or some evening during the week. Many students work for an organization that is easily accessible from their term-time address. Alternatively you can find something in your home town during the holidays.

Obviously, if you manage to get experience in an industry that you might want to work in later, you will have a tremendous advantage when you graduate, as you will have built up valuable knowledge, and most importantly, contacts. However, many of the skills you pick up at work can be applied in a huge range of jobs – it is down to you to explain to potential employers how they are relevant and how you have developed as a person.

Check your answers at the end of this unit (pp. 111–14) before you read the commentary below.

Commentary

The differences between the texts can be explained in terms of the purpose of each one and the type of relationship the writer attempts to establish with the reader. Text 23 is intended as a kind of instruction manual, therefore it is laid out as a list, and the language is direct and straightforward, using a simple pattern of verbs in the imperative.

Texts 24 and 25 are written as responses to specific questions, and so require more complex and varied grammatical structures. Also, as a real or supposed interlocutor is addressed, a list of imperatives, as in Text 23, would have been too impersonal. These texts use imperatives only sparingly, preferring instead a variety of modal verbs with *you*, general statements and *if*-clauses. Text 25 is the least 'directive' of the three: it uses fewer modals expressing strong obligation, and more *if*-clauses to discuss different options. This is because of the nature of the questions. In Text 24 the writer asks for specific advice on how to enter a particular profession, therefore the answers are more straightforward. The questions in Text 25 address more general issues, and therefore demand more differentiated replies and explanations.

WRITTEN AND SPOKEN PROCEDURAL GENRES

Activity

Look back at the activity and commentary on Text 16: Sorting Invoices in Unit four, in which a supervisor trains a new assistant, and then answer the following questions:

◎   What differences can you find between the way advice is given in the three written texts we have just looked at, and the way the supervisor, Ann, gives instructions in Text 16: Sorting Invoices? Look in particular at the use of imperatives and modal verbs.

◎   How would you explain these differences?

Commentary

Compared to the writers of the written procedural texts, the instruction-giver in the spoken text uses far fewer imperatives and modal verbs expressing obligation. Instead she uses more indirect ways of giving instructions, including the use of other modal verbs (e.g. *you can*, *you wanna*) and references to joint action (*we wanna*, *let's*).

These differences can be explained both in terms of the mode (written versus spoken) and the relationship that exists between the writer or speaker and reader or listener. The relationship between the writer and the reader in the texts giving advice to job seekers is quite a distant one. First of all, it is a constructed rather than a 'real' relationship, in that the writer can only assume that the addressed reader is in fact a job seeker who will benefit from the advice. There is obviously no direct relationship between reader and writer, and there is maximal social distance between them, as the writer has the role of expert, while the reader is assumed to be a novice (a graduate with no work experience). In this role of expert, the writer can presume the right to 'dish out' advice in a fairly direct manner. Even so, we saw that there were some differences between the three texts depending on the purpose of each one.

In the spoken text, however, the instruction-giver, Ann, addresses a co-worker, Meg, with whom she works on a regular basis and shares common workplace goals. Although she is Meg's superior and has the authority to tell her what to do, she seems to see her role not so much as a boss handing down directives, but as a co-worker explaining jobs and procedures they are both involved in.

But most of all, it is the situation of being in a face-to-face encounter which demands that speakers take into account the relational aspects of the interaction. This is not to say that there is no relationship between reader and writer in written texts (even if only a constructed one), but as we saw in Unit five, speakers are centrally concerned with politeness and avoiding or mitigating face-threatening acts. This means that although written and spoken procedural texts share some common characteristics (e.g. similar types of modal verbs), they can be quite different, especially in terms of how forcefully and directly instructions, directives or advice are given.

JOB ADVERTISEMENTS

The usual way of looking for a job is to look through job advertisements in newspapers or on websites for positions you would be interested in and you think you are qualified for. Organizations advertising vacant positions are of course hoping to attract the right kind of applicant through their advertisements; and understanding the language of advertisements will help you present yourself in a suitable manner in your application.

Activity

Look at the following two job advertisements from the *Guardian*'s 'Jobs and Money' section, and answer the following questions:

◎ Based on these two texts, what would you say are the essential elements or 'moves' (see Unit three) of the genre of job advertisements?

◎ How do the advertisements try to attract the right kind of applicant? In which move or moves does this occur? Make a note of some of the linguistic strategies used to do this.

◎ If you wanted to apply for these jobs, what information about yourself would you include?

Text 26a: Job Advertisement – Recruitment Consultant

Recruitment Consultant Opportunities

Venn Group
Recruitment Solutions

" Within 10 months of starting recruitment at Venn Group I had full responsibility for my own team. I firmly believe there is no other consultancy in London that could have given me this accelerated career progression. "

Robert McLeod, Aged 26. Joined Venn Group March 2001. Promoted to Team Leader November 2001.

Formed as recently as October 2000, Venn Group is one of the UK and Ireland's fastest-growing recruitment consultancies with offices already established in 6 locations. We specialise in placing temporary and contract staff in the Accountancy, Financial, Legal and IT sectors.

We are currently looking for articulate, persuasive, sales-focussed individuals who want to work for a young, vibrant company with exciting expansion plans. Some previous sales experience would be a distinct advantage but is not essential. We welcome applications from 2003 graduates.

Highly competitive salary packages are available commensurate with experience.

If you, like Robert, want to develop a superb career at Venn Group please call our Recruitment Co-ordinator Ted Edwards on 020 7557 7667 or email your details to tededwards@venngroup.com.

For more information visit our website at www.venngroup.com

LONDON • BRISTOL • LEICESTER • SLOUGH • DUBLIN

Text 26b: Job Advertisement – Flight Centre

Check your answers at the end of this unit (pp. 114–16) before you read the commentary below.

Commentary

Job advertisements have a great deal in common as a genre with the sales promotion letters, which we looked at in Unit three. In the same way as sales promotion letters, their function is persuasive (to get the right people to apply for the job) and many of the moves are similar. In both genres, the organization needs to establish its credentials, and both solicit a response from the reader.

109

The advertisements are written in such a way as to attract the right kind of applicant. Both advertisements are aimed at graduates with little or no previous experience, and the language is meant to appeal to this type of applicant. Besides having positive, upbeat vocabulary (see answers), both advertisements are written in a direct, personal style, addressing the reader with the second person pronoun *you*. The second advertisement uses noticeably informal language, including a number of contractions (*we're*, *we'll*) and some colloquialisms (*bags of energy*).

Job advertisements also reveal a great deal about the type of candidate sought, and reading them carefully can help you present yourself in the right way when you apply. If you wanted to apply for the jobs advertised in both advertisements, you would probably present yourself in a slightly different way for each one. It would be important for both jobs to show that you are ambitious, enthusiastic and a good communicator. The Venn Group advertisement says that sales experience is not essential, but would be a *distinct advantage*. Therefore it would be important to flag up any sales experience, even summer jobs, or at least show an interest in and willingness to learn about sales. The Flight Centre job is also in sales, but the advertisement specifically stresses the importance of travel rather than sales experience. So it would be important to show some geographical knowledge, especially of popular tourist destinations, and to have something interesting to say about your previous travels.

SUMMARY

This final unit has examined texts related to the job search, and two types of texts were analysed in detail:

◎   texts giving advice to job seekers;

◎   job advertisements.

As procedural genres, the advice texts all have a number of things in common (e.g. the use of imperatives and modal verbs), but there are also some differences, depending on the purpose of each text and the type of relationship the writer attempts to establish with the reader. Spoken procedural texts are again different from written ones due to the relational politeness aspects that come into play in face-to-face encounters.

Job advertisements have a characteristic move structure, and have a great deal in common with other persuasive genres such as sales promotional letters.

In keeping with the theme of this book, the principal focus of this unit has been on understanding the language of the texts examined. However, it is hoped that these texts and activities will provide some food for thought for your own job search.

Extension

1   This unit began by looking at texts giving advice about the job hunt. Perhaps you have had some experience yourself with this, having applied for some jobs already, had some interviews, or even had work experience. Based on any experience you have, what advice would you give to someone applying for a job for the first time? Write a text of about 300 words. Include advice on any of the following: the job search, the application procedure, the interview.

2   Look at the job advertisements section of a newspaper, and choose four advertisements for one type of job (for example Creative, Media & Sales) and four advertisements for another type of job (e.g. IT). Analyse the move structure and language of the two sets of advertisements. Are there any noticeable differences and how could you explain them?

ANSWERS TO THE ACTIVITIES

Answers for Texts 23, 24 and 25: Help with the Job Hunt
(pp. 103–5)

◉   **What is the format of each text and why do you think this format was chosen?**

Text 23: Ready for Lift Off, begins like a standard newspaper article, with a subtitle under the title; but after a prose introduction, the rest of the article is laid out as a numbered list of instructions grouped under different headings: *the job search*, *the CV* (other headings not shown are *the covering letter*, *the interview*). The article addresses university graduates in general, but the introductory paragraph also attempts to address them as individuals: here readers are invited to identify with the situation described – having difficulty concentrating on the job search now that summer is here. However, as the aim of the article is to provide a useful set of guidelines for the job search, a straightforward, schematic layout is chosen.

Text 24: Ask Rise uses an 'Agony Aunt' format, where readers can write in with questions, and selected questions are then printed together with the expert's answer. The answer is addressed to the reader who sent in the letter, but it is assumed that it will interest other readers as well. This 'dialogic' form of advice giving is clearly intended to appeal to readers, as people are always interested in others' individual problems.

Text 25: Work Experience FAQs uses a 'frequently asked questions' format, which is quite commonly used for advice-giving texts, particularly on websites. As in Text 24, it uses a dialogic format of question and answer, but it is a constructed dialogue, as we do not really know if anyone has actually asked these questions. By using this format, the writer attempts to set out the advice in a way that will seem relevant to the readers' own situations, as it is assumed they would have questions like this.

All three texts address the reader using the second person *you*, and so try to make the general advice they give to relevant to individual readers.

◎ **How does each text give advice?**

◎ **How can you account for the differences between the texts?**

Text 23 uses imperatives throughout. Each point in the list begins with a verb in the imperative:

◎ <u>Take</u> responsibility

◎ <u>Start</u> a daily log

◎ <u>Take</u> control

Text 24 uses only one imperative:

◎ <u>Put</u> yourself inside the recruiter's head

but instead employs a number of modal verbs expressing obligation or necessity:

◎ you'll <u>have to</u>

- ◎   you <u>must</u> (used twice)
- ◎   you <u>should</u>
- ◎   this <u>needs</u> to be

The writer also gives advice by making some general statements in the present tense:

- ◎   Everything is possible
- ◎   Some recruiters . . . Others . . .
- ◎   Many companies . . .
- ◎   <u>The most effective way</u> of acquiring that is . . .

Of all the texts, Text 25 employs the greatest range of devices for giving advice. Again there is only one imperative (*Remember*) and a number of modal verbs, but only two modals of obligation/necessity:

- ◎   you will <u>need</u>
- ◎   you <u>don't have to</u>

Note that the second one in fact indicates lack of obligation, and that we find no modals expressing strong obligation (*must, should, have to*), unlike in Text 24. Other modal verbs make predictions about the future:

- ◎   you <u>will</u> be
- ◎   you <u>will</u> have built up

or indicate possibilities and options :

- ◎   can (used four times)
- ◎   <u>may</u> be
- ◎   you <u>might</u> (used twice)

These modals are often used in *if*-clauses in discussing different options and possibilities, for example:

- ◎   Obviously, if you manage to get experience in an industry that <u>you might want to</u> work in later, <u>you will have</u> a tremendous advantage when you graduate, as you <u>will have</u> built up . . .

As in Text 24, general statements in the present tense are also used:

◎ Employers are increasingly demanding that . . .

◎ Many students work . . .

Finally, the writer uses a number of fixed, idiomatic expressions for advice giving:

◎ It's never too early (a variation on 'it's never too late')

◎ you don't have long

◎ it's down to you

◎ so much the better

Answers for Texts 26a and 26b: Job Advertisements (pp. 108–9)

The following moves seem to be essential ingredients in job advertisements, although the order may vary:

1 Establishing credentials/introducing the employer:

26a: Formed as recently as October 2000, Venn Group is one of the UK and Ireland's fastest-growing recruitment consultancies . . . .

26b: (This does not occur in the actual text, but there are two vignettes in the headline which establish the credentials of the company):

2 Giving profile of applicant sought:

26a: We are currently looking for articulate, persuasive, sales-focussed individuals . . . We welcome applications from 2003 graduates.

26b: When we're looking for Graduates to join us here at Flight Centre, we consider the subject of their degree less important . . . Bring us this, together with bags of energy and enthusiasm

3 Describing benefits of the job:

26a: Highly competitive salary packages are available commensurate with experience.

This is also done by using the example of the employee Robert McLeod:

◎ Within 10 months of starting recruitment at Venn Group . . .

◎ If you, like Robert, want to develop a superb career

26b: . . . we'll introduce you to an exciting sales career with fantastic long-term prospects . . . And to keep indulging your passion for travel, we'll give you generous discounts on all the products we sell.

4 Giving information about application procedure:

This comes at the end of both advertisements:

26a: . . . please call our Recruitment Co-ordinator . . .

26b: If you wish to attend our Careers Day . . .

Another move often found in job advertisements not included in these two is a description of the duties of the position.

◎ How do the advertisements try to attract the right kind of applicant?

The moves 'Establishing credentials' and 'Describing benefits of the job' both have the primary function of 'selling' the company to the applicant. Note the use of positive vocabulary in 'Establishing credentials', in particular superlative adjectives:

fastest-growing (26a)

best (26b)

The benefits of the job described in both advertisements include salary and promotion prospects. Text 26a also mentions other benefits , including a personal trainer and financial adviser, as well as discounts for travel. The quote from an employee in Text 26a is of course supposed to lend credibility to the claim that 'accelerated career progression' is possible. Again, very positive vocabulary is used, in particular evaluative adjectives:

Text 26a:

highly competitive salary packages

superb career

Text 26b:

<u>exciting</u> sales career with <u>fantastic</u> long-term prospects

<u>generous</u> discounts

While the principal function of the move 'Giving profile of applicant sought' is to let prospective applicants know if they have the correct profile, even here the advertisement aims to attract applicants by describing the person sought in very positive terms:

articulate, persuasive, sales-focussed individuals (26a)

bags of energy and enthusiasm . . . a real high flier (26b)

references and further reading

REFERENCES

Bhatia, V. K. (1993) *Analysing Genre: Language Use in Professional Settings*, London: Longman.

Brown, P. and Levinson, S. (1987*) Politeness: Some Universals in Language Usage*, Cambridge: Cambridge University Press.

Cameron, D. (2000) *Good to Talk? Living and Working in a Communication Culture*, London: Sage.

Carter, R. and McCarthy, M. (1997) *Exploring Spoken English*, Cambridge: Cambridge University Press.

Cheepen, C. (2000) 'Small talk in service dialogues: the conversational aspects of transactional telephone talk', in J. Coupland (ed.), *Small Talk*, Harlow: Pearson Education, pp. 288–311.

Devitt, A. (1991) 'Intertextuality in tax accounting: generic, referential and functional', in C. Bazerman and J. Paradis (eds), *Textual Dynamics of the Professions*, Madison, WI: University of Wisconsin Press, pp. 336–57.

Drew, P. and Heritage, J. (eds) (1992) *Talk at Work*, Cambridge: Cambridge University Press.

Heath, C. (1992) 'The delivery and reception of diagnosis in the general-practice consultation', in P. Drew and J. Heritage (eds), *Talk at Work*, Cambridge: Cambridge University Press, pp. 235–67.

Hoey, M. (2001) *Textual Interaction: An Introduction to Written Discourse Analysis*, London: Routledge.

Louhiala-Salminen, L. (1999) 'From business correspondence to message exchange: what is left?', in M. Hewings and C. Nickerson (eds), *Business English: Research into Practice*, Harlow: Longman, pp. 100–14.

McCarthy, M. and Carter, R. (2000) 'Feeding back: non-minimal response tokens in everyday English conversation', in C. Heffer and H. Sauntson (eds), *Words in Context: A Tribute to John Sinclair on his Retirement*, Birmingham: University of Birmingham.

Moon, R. (1992) 'Textual aspects of fixed expressions in learners' dictionaries', in P. Arnaud and H. Béjoint (eds), *Vocabulary and Applied Linguistics*, London: Macmillan, pp. 13–27.

Swales, J. M. (1990) *Genre Analysis: English in Academic and Research Settings*, Cambridge: Cambridge University Press.

Winter, E. (1994) 'Clause relations as information structure: two basic text structures in English', in M. Coulthard (ed.), *Advances in Written Text Analysis*, London: Routledge, pp. 46–68.

FURTHER READING

For a more in-depth discussion of the notions of discourse community and genre see:

Swales, J. M. (1990) *Genre Analysis: English in Academic and Research Settings*, Cambridge: Cambridge University Press.

The following book looks at a number of legal and business genres, dealing specifically with sales promotion letters and job applications:

Bhatia, V. K. (1993) *Analysing Genre: Language Use in Professional Settings*, London: Longman.

A classic book on workplace talk, which provides a theoretical foundation, as well as in-depth analysis of interactions from many different workplace settings (including clinical, legal and journalistic) is:

Drew, P. and Heritage, J. (eds) (1992) *Talk at Work*, Cambridge: Cambridge University Press.

If you are interested in English language teaching, the following book reports studies of different written and spoken business genres and discusses their relevance for teaching:

Hewings, M. and Nickerson, C. (eds) (1999) *Business English: Research into Practice*, Harlow: Longman.

The following three books provide a cross-cultural perspective on business language. The first, by Hostede, is a classic work, which is the foundation for a great deal of current thinking on cultural differences, and the second is a collection of case studies across a number of different cultures, and the third is a handbook for language teachers:

Hofstede, G. (1990) *Culture's Consequences: International Differences in Work-Related Values*, London: Sage.

Bargiela-Chiappini, F. and Harris, S. J. (eds) (1997) *The Language of Business: An International Perspective*, Edinburgh: Edinburgh University Press.

Gibson, R. (2002) *Intercultural Business Communication*, Oxford: Oxford University Press.

A book which takes a critical view of the 'communication culture', particularly in the workplace is:

Cameron, D. (2000) *Good to Talk? Living and Working in a Communication Culture*, London: Sage.

For a popularized account of gender differences in workplace talk see:

Tannen, D. (1994) *Talking from 9 to 5: How Men and Women's Conversational Style Affect Who Gets Heard, Who Gets Credit, and What Gets Done at Work*, New York: William and Morrow.

A good source for recent studies of workplace discourse and discussions of issues related to teaching English for professional purposes is the international journal *English for Specific Purposes* published by Elsevier Science, now also available on the internet at www.sciencedirect.com.

index of terms

agenda 9

A list of the topics to be discussed at a meeting, which is circulated beforehand to the participants. The first item on the agenda is usually apologies for the people who cannot attend the meeting, followed by the **minutes** of the last meeting, and final items are 'Any Other Business' (or AOB) and the date of the next meeting.

back channelling 79

Feedback provided by listeners to show comprehension or interest while someone is speaking: for example, *yeah, mhm, really.* (*See also* **minimal response**).

context 34

The language occurring before or after a word, utterance or stretch of text. The context can also be the broader social situation within which a text occurs, including **shared knowledge** of the speakers/listeners or writers/ readers.

discourse 1

A term used in linguistics to describe the rules and conventions underlying the use of language in extended stretches of **text**, spoken and written. It is also used as a convenient general term to refer to language in action and the patterns which characterize particular types of language in action; for example, the 'discourse' of advertising.

discourse community 15

A professional, academic or other social group with a common set of goals, mechanisms of intercommunication and one or more genres, which it uses in pursuing its aims. Discourse communities can be very large, for example an international community of academics or scientists within a particular area of research, or much smaller, such as a group of co-workers within an organization.

discourse markers 60

Words like *and, so, but, then* which show how different parts of the **discourse** relate to one another. They are often used to mark a change of topic or some kind of shift in the direction of the conversation.

face 85

Positive face is the positive self-image one wishes to present, including the desire that this self-image be appreciated. Negative face is the claim to freedom of action and freedom from imposition. Much interaction involves **face-threatening acts** – the danger that positive or negative face may be lost. Through 'face-work', i.e. by using **politeness** strategies, speakers try to reduce the impact of face-threatening acts. *See also* Unit five.

face-threatening act (*see* **face**) 85

genre 7

Any set of communicative events (spoken or written) that have the same communicative purpose and typically share certain recurring features, such as the same underlying structure, and can therefore be recognized as belonging to the same type. Some genres are common to many different areas of work (e.g. meetings, job interviews, business letters), whereas others are specific to particular professions (e.g., cross-examinations, medical records). *See also* Unit one.

hedges 96

Words or phrases which soften or weaken the force with which something is said. Hedges are typically adverbs, such as *just*, *quite*, *really*, *sort of*, which have very little meaning on their own.

idiom 96

A sequence of words which functions as a single unit of meaning and which cannot normally be interpreted literally. For example, 'She is over the moon' contains the idiom 'over the moon' meaning 'happy'.

intertextuality 34

The way in which one text echoes or refers to another text. For example, an advertisement which stated 'To be in Florida in winter, or not to be in Florida in winter' would contain an intertextual reference to a key speech in Shakespeare's *Hamlet*. *See also* Unit three.

intonation xi

This refers to a number of different features relating to the sounds of spoken language: the way people raise and lower their pitch, stress certain syllables and vary their speech rhythm.

invoice 30

A bill sent or given to a customer for the sale of goods or services.

lexis 2

The vocabulary system of a language. The type of lexis used varies depending on whether a **text** is written or spoken, and what the **genre** or **register** is. Specialized or technical lexis is often used in specific professions or workplaces.

matching contrast 23

A matching contrast relationship describes the kind of link established between two clauses or sentences by repeating some items (for example, items of vocabulary or grammatical structures) and contrasting others (for example, by using antonyms). This is a device used by writers in order to set up some kind of opposition between two things or highlight differences (*see* Hoey 2001 and Winter 1994).

memo 29

A memo (or memorandum) is a brief official piece of written communication circulated to everybody within an organization or in a particular department. Memos are used, for example, to announce changes within the organization or to remind members of staff to take some action.

metalanguage 6

Language used to talk about language or to describe particular instances of speech or writing.

If you say 'We had an interesting conversation', the word *conversation* is metalinguistic.

minimal response 80

A type of **back channelling** that gives the minimum amount of feedback required from a listener to acknowledge understanding or show that the channel of communication remains open. Examples of minimal responses are *okay, mm, mhm, yes, yeah, right*. (*See also* **non-minimal response**.)

minutes 9

A written record of what was discussed at a meeting. One participant, usually a secretary, takes the minutes during the meeting and later writes them up and circulates them to the participants.

modal verbs 62

Also called 'modal auxiliaries', these are verbs such as *must, may, can, will, could, should*. Modals show the speaker's or writer's attitude, for example how certain the person feels about something. For instance, saying 'It will rain', means you are fairly sure, whereas 'It may rain' indicates that you have some doubt.

non-minimal response 80

A type of **back channelling** where listeners produce more than a **minimal response** to show understanding. This includes expressions such as *lovely, great, that's true*, which show interest, agreement, enthusiasm or other attitudes and emotions. *See also* Unit five.

order 30

A request for goods or services from a **supplier** who sells these.

politeness 85

Interactive strategies used to maintain self and others' **face**. Politeness strategies are addressed either to positive or negative face. Positive politeness strategies include compliments, praise, avoiding criticism, showing appreciation and claiming common ground. Negative politeness strategies include apologizing, not being presumptuous, using **hedges** and making indirect requests. *See also* Unit five.

procedural 66

A written or spoken **genre** which involves giving instructions or explaining a procedure can be described as 'procedural'. Examples of written procedural genres are recipes and instruction manuals. *See also* Units four and six.

quotation 30

A quotation or quote is the price a customer is told in advance that some goods or services will cost.

register 7

The set of linguistic features which characterizes texts in different professional and academic fields, as well as other specific contexts. These linguistic features include grammar, **lexis**, as well as **style**. Examples of registers are the language of journalism or the language of advertising. Register is not the same thing as **genre**. Registers are used to construct genres, but genres themselves are completed **texts** or activities.

service encounter 88

A conversation in which a service provider interacts with a customer or member of the public requesting or receiving some goods or services.

Service encounters typically involve interactions in shops, post offices and banks, or telephone conversations with a variety of service providers. *See also* Unit five.

shared knowledge 34

Background knowledge common to all participants in a conversation or writers and readers of a text. Shared knowledge may result from having had previous contact, working or living together or simply from sharing the same culture. The more shared knowledge participants have, the less explicit they need to be in what they say or write.

social distance 10

The relative degree of social difference between two people, for example in terms of status, power, class or ethnic origin.

style 8

Variation in a person's speech or writing from casual to formal.

Style can also refer to a person's individual way of speaking or writing.

supplier 63

A company or person who sells materials, products or services to a business, for example a manufacturer or a retail shop.

text 6

A piece of spoken or written language of any length (from a single word to a sermon or novel). Both **text** and **discourse** can be used to refer to oral *or* written communication.

turn-taking 2

The phenomenon that in conversation the roles of speaker and listener alternate, that is people 'take turns' at speaking. The rules for turn-taking may differ from one community to another and certain types of workplace talk have special turn-taking rules.